Exercises in the 23rd Edition of the DEWEY DECIMAL CLASSIFICATION

Melvil Dewey (1851-1931)

Exercises in the 23rd Edition of the

DEWEY DECIMAL CLASSIFICATION

By
M P Satija
UGC Emeritus Fellow
GURU NANAK DEV UNIVERSITY

Ess Ess Publications

4837/24, Ansari Road, Darya Ganj,
New Delhi-110002
✆ : 23260807, 41563444
Fax : 011-41563334
E-mail: info@essessreference.com
url:http://www.essessreference.com

First Edition 2012

Published by SUMIT SETHI
for **Ess Ess Publications**
4837/24, Ansari Road, Darya Ganj,
New Delhi - 110 002
Ph. : 23260807, 41563444
Fax : 011-41563334
E-mail: info@essessreference.com
url:http://www.essessreference.com

ISBN : 978-81-7000-669-5

Price : Rs. 325/-

Laser Typesetting:
Mukesh Graphics
T-1264, Mangolpuri, New Delhi
Ph. : 9899079035, 27918550
E-mail:mukeshgraphics29@gmail.com

Printed at :
Print Line

People donate money to religious places to secure a niche in Heaven for themselves.

Here are a few NRIs:

Dr. JASWANT SINGH, Er. BALDEV SINGH DHALIWAL and Mr. JOGINDER SINGH KALSI

spending their hard earned money to create heaven for others on this earth by establishing rural libraries in their villages in Punjab.
To them and their ilk this book is dedicated.
May their tribe increase

Contents

Preface

"It's a big world. We've organised it." - **OCLC**

A system of library classification whose technique flashed across the inquiring mind of young Melvil Dewey (1851-1931) on a fine May morning in 1873 is still the most popular one the world over. Soon after its publication in 1876, its popularity spread across the globe. At present, it is estimated to be used in 2 lakh libraries and information centres in about 130 countries in six continents. Sixty two national or trade bibliographies are arranged by the DDC. The sun never sets on the DDC empire. Now it is trying to find many uses outside the library, e.g., organizing and retrieval information on the Internet and in knowledge networks. Even a hotel is now organised on Dewey's Decimal System.* Not only this, the invention of the DDC has played a vital role in giving direction and shape to modern librarianship. It is not for nothing that Melvil Dewey is given the title: Father of modern librarianship!

Historically speaking, modern library classification begins with the DDC. It provided a paradigm to all the library classification systems that have come up in its wake. Classification by discipline (also depicting hierarchic relations), ingenious use of decimal notation, and the relative index are its enduring contributions which have been borrowed by all the later classifications as their very basis.

Some have improved upon it in some ways but faltered in others. None could catch up with its popularity and simplicity, however. Despite criticism of its 19th century structure, its popularity has always shown an ascending graph. Popularity is based upon simplicity and efficacy.

Revision of the DDC is institutionalised, and so is a continuous process. It has undergone constant revisions to keep itself abreast of the ever advancing frontiers of knowledge and to cater to the increasing demand of its users. The 24th edition is presently under way. In every revision, it is expanded, modified, rectified, and made more modern in its methods and outlook and format. Since Dewey, it has come a long way in its endeavours to meet the needs of society overwhelmed by the information revolution. It has been translated into about 35 major languages of the world, ranging from Vietnamese, Hebrew, Arabic, Hindi and Thai to French, German, Italian, Spanish and Russian. Translations are planned and aided by the "International Dewey Users Meeting" held annually at the IFLA world conference. In many countries, its relevant portions have been recast and expanded to suit their local needs. Some of such adaptations and home-made expansions are officially recognised. The system is taught in library schools all over the world.

Yet many librarians criticise it for its enumerative pattern. The criticism is now only partially valid. They plead to abandon it or not to adopt it but fail to provide a better alternative. Frustrated, they declare classification as an impossibility or absurdity. Many a critical storm has raged to uproot it. Always it has come out unscathed. At times, it was forsaken by some to be readopted later. Deserters had to comeback to its fold, eventually. Once declared dead, it is now pulsating with a vigorous life. It is living and kicking and is a very influencing system in many ways. The system has been modernised and geared up to play its role in the Information Society of the 21st century.

Notwithstanding the fashion to criticise it, the system has become the very marrow in the bones that a librarian make. It has become an institution of librarianship as it now involves many shades of the community of librarians in its making. It is the only gateway to learn the theory and practice of library classification; and for many it is the end. For many others, the DDC means the classification.

One of the repeated charge is that having no philosophy of its own, it is not based on any theory. This is only partially true. Nevertheless, the DDC is a practical scheme that answers the basic problems of classifying and organising information in libraries.

The DDC has over the years given rise to many interesting and revealing theoretical studies. A good part of total classification literature is exclusively devoted to this system. It invariably constitutes a central chapter in any book on library classification. Examples are cited from its schedules to show classification methods. Some of its studies have shed light on the socio-politico-cultural bearings of classification. It has been a subject of some doctoral dissertations, many research projects and exclusive conferences and workshops. The tide of literature on the DDC is constantly swelling.

In the 23rd edition released in May 2011, the DDC has been further modernised both conceptually and physically. It has been simultaneously made available in traditional print edition (of 4 volumes)) and electronic through the Internet called WebDewey 2.0. It is a hi tech but user friendly edition which has more and clear notes, more interdisciplinary numbers, improved and enhanced relative index and an expanded Manual. The manual entries are also included in the relative index. Vocabulary reflects international usage. Internationalisation and users' convenience are its hallmarks.

The present book aims to introduce the students to the process of assigning class numbers by the 23rd edition of the DDC. The Chapters and the examples have been graded to some extent. No background, whatsoever, has been assumed on the part of the reader. Though it aims at the beginner, yet it provides a complete course to train the students in the techniques of number building involving the use of various auxiliary tables and multiple synthesis. A chapter each has been devoted to the structure of the DDC and subject analysis of the documents to be classified.

Alternative class numbers have also been given whenever official options allow. The graded process of number building may mirror before the students the increasing faceted nature of the system and its advancing steps towards what S.R. Ranganathan terms as depth classification. To avoid long discussions the number building has been depicted through equations and facet formulas. This may mentally stimulate-the students. It is hoped that in this way the student will learn the ropes of the DDC through this how-to-do-it text.

In this edition new examples have been added from revised classes of 004-006 Data processing (in computer science), 160 Logic, 200 Religion, 305-306 Social groups and institutions, 340 Law, 510 Mathematics especially 518 Numerical analysis, and 610 Medicine. The chapter on the Relative Index has been simplified. The examples, chosen of necessity, are largely imaginary, though not far from the realities of literary warrant. The aim is to be amply illustrative and to introduce step-by-step all the concepts and methods of the DDC. In the process some repetition was inevitable, for which the forbearance of the readers is sought. Another aim is to be simple and clear. It is admitted that to write simply has been as simple and difficult as writing on "how to lace a shoe".

The book is based on the 23rd edition of the DDC. But it is expected that an intelligent student is able to adapt this book to other recent editions.

Suggestions for improvement are earnestly requested.

M P S
satija_mp@yahoo.com

NOTES

The **Library Hotel**, New York <www.libraryhotel.com>is a 60-room *boutique hotel* in *New York City*, located at 299 *Madison Avenue* (at 41st Street), near the *New York Public Library*, *Bryant Park*, and *Grand Central Terminal*. The hotel boasts a unique organizing principle: each of its ten guest floors has a theme, designated after a major category of the *Dewey Decimal Classification* (the 5th floor, for example, is the 500s, the Sciences), with each room as a subcategory or genre, such as *Mathematics* (Room 500.001) or *Botany* (Room 500.004). (Dewey categories 000, 100, and 200 are placed on the 10th, 11th, and 12th floors, respectively.) Other room themes include *Erotic Literature* (Room 800.001), *Poetry* (Room 800.003), and *Music* (Room 700.005). All rooms have a small complement of books and decorations that accompany the theme, with 6000 books overall throughout the hotel. Because of this classification scheme, the hotel owners were sued in 2003 by the *OCLC*. Later the OCLC reached an agreement with the hotel enabling it to continue using the Dewey system. (Wikipedia)

BUBL LINK *http://bubl.ac.uk/link/*, catalogue of selected Internet resources covering all academic subject areas, uses the Dewey Decimal Classification system as the primary organisation structure for its catalogue

Acknowledgement

Thanks are to Dr K P Singh, his students Malkeet Singh and Harish Arora for their help in the enormous and tedious task of proof reading this book. Thanks are also due to Dr Manoj K Joshi for his valuable suggestions, and last but not the least to many students and teachers, Professor P. Ranasinghe of Kelaniya University, Sri Lanka outstanding among them, for their encouraging and constructive suggestions on the previous edition of this book. Last but not the least to Professor Gurpartap Singh Khairah who served me as a language expert to use the correct idiom in the book.

M P S

Salient Features of the 23rd Edition (2011)

The 23rd edition of the DDC, earlier scheduled to be published in 2010, was delayed about a year to be released in May 2011 in the 135th year of its first publication in 1876. That small pamphlet published anonymously very soon puck like girdled the world, as if it was being awaited. Since then, save a brief period of 1950s, it has been on an ascending path of progress scaling new heights and covering new territories at home and abroad. Though counted among the big three library classification systems (the other two being the UDC and the (LCC), it has surpassed them in its popularity, simplicity and use. Now it is well entrenched in Europe too where since 2007 "European DDC User Group" (EDUG) has been officially established. Used in about two lac libraries in 130 countries in six continents, and in sixty two national and trade bibliographies, its official translations exist or are under way in more than thirty major languages of the world. It has found many uses in electronic databases, organising and retrieving information on the web, as an online management tool, supporting collection developments, mapping thesauri and subject schemes. The WorldCat/OCLC, the largest ever bibliographic database, uses the DDC. The OCLC since its acquisition of the DDC in 1988 has given an impetus to research in wider applications of the DDC especially in the digital environment. The Knowledge Organization Group in OCLC Research first under Diane Vizine-Goetz and now Lorcan Dempsey has made substantial advances in this area. From its founding aim of arranging books and pamphlets on library shelves it is now at the center of research in theory and practice of knowledge organization and information retrieval. No wonder for many a layperson the classification means the DDC.

The 23rd edition, of all its half a dozen recent editions, has come with minimum changes. There is nothing to speak of any major change except updating of schedules here and there. The entire gamut of changes (as listed on pages xxv-xlii, Vol.1) fills only eighteen pages. "…. expansion and revision have been preferred to relocation" states the chairperson of the DCEPC Ms Caroline Kent (Vol. 1, p. xi.). This time its thrust seems on marketing by associating experts and users from different libraries and countries. The present chair of the Dewey Decimal Classification Editorial Policy Committee (DCEPC) Caroline Kent is from the British Library. It is for the first time that a non-American is occupying this influential chair. And it is for the first time that a member (Welna van Eeden) has been taken from South Africa on the DCEPC. A very active and strongly organized group EDUG has been established to promote the use of DDC in Europe, initiate translations in European languages and the need for research in their interoperability and discuss problems of translation and practical use in those countries. International Dewey Users Meeting is a group of translators, which helps to improve its international usage. A long list of institutions, individuals and groups who offered advice on updates has been given in acknowledgement. Thirty four individuals have been acknowledged for their advise only on updating 741.5 Comic books, graphic novels, fotonovelas, cartoons, caricatures and comic strips. Apart from additions the new edition updates terminology "to improve currency and accessibilities for classifier". It is asserted that the changes have been motivated by classifiers efficiency and emerging requirements in machine representation and application (New features, p. xxi, vol1).

Some of the proclaimed changes are:

004-006 Computer sciences, and parallel provisions in 621.39 Computer engineering, and 025.04 Information storage and retrieval.

155 differential and development psychology.

160 & 513 Logic and Symbolic logic.

In 200 Religion updates have been initiated for 281.9 Orthodox church and 297 Islam which will also be continued in the 24th edition. There are minor changes, addition and terminological updating in 300-390 Social sciences, and a few more languages have been added in Table 6, and corresponding additions in 400 and 800 schedules have been incorporated. Of interest to Indians may be the following numbers:

491.489 Divehi (Maldivian language)

491.492 Eastern Hindi languages

491.496 Pahari languages

Number for dialects (geographic variations) of many languages such as Swedish, Danish, Finnish, Norwegian, French, Italian, Spanish, Portuguese (may be under the influence of EDUG) and Chinese language have been provided. New forms of art, graphic arts, graphic novels, comic books, etc. have been relocated from 760 to 740. Obviously history dates and areas in schedules and tables have been updated.

There are some structural and terminological changes of no consequence to the end user, through claimed to increase the efficiency of classifiers and to facilitate machine display and retrieval. The present edition is now a byproduct of the online WebDewey 2.0 released simultaneously. WebDewey 2.0 has been prepared using 4th generation of the Editorial Support System (ESS 4.0, 2010). New data format is now based on open source MARC21, and formats for Classification and Authority Data. WebDewey is now the chief vehicle for delivering monthly updates. Unwieldy headings for the three main summaries have been edited to make them handy. For example 500 Natural Sciences and mathematics appear simply as Science. 600 Technology (Applied Science) appears as only Technology in the first Summary. 320 Political science (politics and government) appear only as 320 Political science in the second summary. Then in the Table 1-08 kinds of person has been renamed as Groups of People with corresponding changes in the schedules of 155 Differential psychology, 305-306 Psychology of social groups, 331 Labour economics, and of course in T1-092 Biography. Then wherever any subdivision in Table 1 is used differently in the schedules, it is indicated so now, otherwise it was quite obvious.

For example,

331.01 Philosophy and theory (of Labour economic)

Motivation 01 from table of as modified below

331.01 Rights and position of labour

331.0112 Industrial democracy.

Also there is elimination of dual headings. For example, in the previous edition some three-digit number had dual headings, both the headings separated by four spaces in the scheduled were given as:

532 Fluid Mechanics	Liquid mechanics
570 Life Sciences	Biology
954 South Asia	India

All such provision are replaced by a single heading, with the other included as the class here note. Now 532 is Fluid mechanics with a note to class Liquid mechanics here. Similarly, 954 is given the heading "[History of] India and neighboring south Asian countries. Such changes are both in schedules and tables. As another structural change uneven span of numbers have been balanced digitally. For example 420.1-428 has been changed to 420.1-420.9 and 421-428. Similarly, 305.805-.89 is now rendered as 305.805-.809 and 305.81-.89. There were only a few such ranges of numbers which however had never posed any challenge or problem even to a very modest DDC classifier, through such transcription of number saved lot of space on the schedules.

Apart from these there is no major change in schedules or grammar of number building. Nor there is any innovation. It seems if the editors have run out of ideas, or has the revision process come a full circle. The vow of integrity of numbers taken in 1885 seems to have been observed only to its best in this edition. In such a situation one wonders, if it was necessary to bring out a new edition. Would not supplement of 20-25 pages have served the purpose, instead. In face of continuously updated WebDewey the edition has lost its strict boundaries, even definition. Nevertheless, the new edition was a necessity, politically, and ritually to renew its life.

Its on going popularity, consequent its thoughtful and grateful dedication to the worldwide Dewey community, its increasing applications in the digital information environment, and its innovative marketing and research machinery keep the system at the top.

Sources

Dewey Decimal Classification and the Relative Index/ devised by Melvil Dewey, 23rd ed./ed. By Joan S. Mitchell; Julianne Beal, *et al*, assistant editors. Dublin, Ohio: OCLC, 2011, 4v. ISBN-13:976-1-910608-81-4 (set)

EDUG http://www.slainte.org.uk/edug/india.htm.

http://www.oclc.org/dewey/

Green, Rebecca, "See also relationship in the Dewey Decimal Classification" *Kng Org.* 38(4)2011:335-341.

025.431 The Dewey blog (*http://www.typepad.com/*).

National Information Standards Organization. *Guideline for the construction, format and management of monolingual controlled vocabularies*: Bethesda, MD: NISO Press, 2005 (ANSI/NISO.Z39.19-2005)

Satija, M.P. *The theory and practice of the DDC*. Oxford, U.K.: Chandos, 2007. Xix, 206p.

1

Introduction to The Text of Four Volumes

Since the 20th edition (1989) the print versions of the DDC (full edition) have continued to be in four volumes.* The four volumes of the DDC 23 forming a total of 4271 pages (DDC 22 had 4076) (including prefatory material) have been organised into four volumes as follows :

The print DDC 23 in four volumes containing 4271 pages in all has been divided into eleven sections marked A/ K as follows:

Volume I, Sections A/G

A	xi-xlii	Prefatory text, notes and new features
B	xliii-lxxi	Introduction to the system of the DDC
C	lxxiii-1xxxii	Glossary : Brief definitions of terms used in the theory and practice of the DDC
D	lxxxiii-lxxxv	Index to the terms and concepts in sections A/C.
E	1-175	Manual : A guide to the interpretation and comprehension of some ambiguous

		numbers; to compare and contrast two analogous or seemingly similar subjects in the schedules and tables.
F	177-761	Six tables with their subdivisions
G	763-779	List that compares Editions 22 and 23 Equivalence table of relocated discontinued and reused numbers from the previous edition

Volume 2, Sections H & I

H	v-xvi	Three Main Summaries
I	1-1291	Schedules of classes 000-599

Volume 3, Section J

J	1-1140	Schedules of classes 600-999

Volume 4, Section K

K	1-965	Relative index : Alphabetical and structured index of subjects and topics listed in context of disciplines and their corresponding numbers in schedules and tables

Volume 1. The first volume of lxxxv + 799 pages contains the prefatory material by the Chair DCEPC (pp. xi-xiii), the "New Features in the Edition 22" (xxi - xlii pages). Introduction (pp. xliii-lxxi) to the DDC is a sort of operational manual including, its theory and philosophy which has been further simplified in this edition. Glossary of terms and concepts (pp. lxiii - lxxxii) used in the preceding chapters is brief explanation of terms used in theory and preface of the DDC. Rest of the pages are devoted to the Manual (pp.1-175), six tables (pp.177-761) and a ready recknor of relocated, discontinued and comparative table of numbers between DDC-22 and 23 (pp. 763 - 779).

Volumes 2 - 3 : These two volumes are devoted to the

schedules of classes. The volume 2 of pages xvi + 1291 lists classes 001 - 599. The schedules are prefaced by three major summaries, namely, Ten Main Classes (First Summary), Hundred Divisions (Second Summary), and Thousand Sections (Third summary). These summaries help to visualise at a glance the mapping and structure of universe of knowledge or its portions as depicted in the DDC. In fact the summaries, both in theory and practice have been so useful that the editors have carried summaries to lower levels (multi level summaries) in the schedules and tables. There are three levels of summaries; the other being the first level summaries. The third volume contains schedules of classes 600 - 999. The classes in the schedules are arranged in 001-999 order, and the Section number is always printed twice on top of every page, as it is more convenient to scan the schedules by class numbers than by page numbers. **Schedules have been defined as "series of numbers constituting the notation for the DDC classes and all their corresponding subject names"**. This is systematic and hierarchical burgeoning of the Ten Main Classes. This may be called the *terra firma* of the system—learning the practice of the DDC is to learn to operate it. Schedules and tables consist of entries. An entry is a unit record which contains a class number on the left, and on its right is given the caption, i.e. the verbal heading for the content of the number. The subordination and coordination relations among the subjects are shown by the length of the class number on the left and the shifting of indention of the captions to the right. In many of the entries there are a variety of notes of explanations and instructions. These notes are essential to assign and build a correct class number, and for inter-indexer consistency.

Volume 4 : Its 965 pages contain the Relative Index (DDC 22 had 928 pages). The Relative Index is considered to be one of the enduring contributions of Melvil Dewey. It is a great help to classifiers, and many prefer to approach the

Schedules through the Index. The Index is called relative as it brings together all aspects of a single topic which have otherwise been scattered by discipline in the Schedules. Hence, Schedules, Tables and the Index are complementary to one another.

TYPES OF ENTRIES

All the approximate 30000+ entries in the schedules may be divided into six categories.

1. **Usable numbers :** Current and in force
2. **Unusable headings :** Not to be used)
3. **Unassigned numbers :** Number without a class
4. **Optional numbers :** Providing alternative numbers
5. **Hook numbers:** A number having no meaning in itself but introduces many examples of the topic
6. Centered heading: A span of numbers for one topic

1. Usable entries

Most of the entries in the system are ordinary entries: a number with a corresponding heading which may or may not have notes or instructions. These are applied numbers.

2. Unusable headings

Consequence of revision, a whole or part of a class number may be relocated to some other place or discontinued. Such a number is enclosed within a square bracket. (See notes 13 and 14 in this chapter i.e. discontinued and relocation notes).

3. Unassigned number

A division or a section in whole may be empty of any topic. These, empty numbers termed as unassigned numbers, are enclosed a square bracket along with a note indicating the edition when it was last used or assigned meaning. For example :

[456] [Unassigned]
Most recently used in Edition 18

It means that section 484 has remained vacant since the 19th edition. A complete list of unassigned Division and Sections in the DDC 23 is given below:

040	376-377	768
Sections	396-397	775
007-009	416	804
013	424	991-992
018	426	
019	434	
024	436	
029	444	
040-049	446	
104	454	
112	456	
125	464	
132	466	
134	474	
136	476	
151	484	
157	486	
159	504	
163	517	
164	524	
216-219	544-545	
237	574	
244-245	589	
256-258	619	
288	626	
291	654-56	
308-309	689	
311-313	699	
329	744	
	756	
	762	

4. Optional numbers

All parenthetical numbers in the schedules are optional offering a choice to libraries to use that or alternative number given in such a type of entry.

Wherever another place for a subject is available, this is indicated with a note "Option : Class with ...". This is an option which is not used by the Dewey Section of the Library of Congress, the official laboratory of the scheme. But if it suits any individual library this option may be availed of. For example, under 016 Subject bibliographies and catalogs, one reads "Option: Class with the specific discipline or subject, using notation 016 from Table 1, e.g., Bibliographies of medicine 610.16". Some critics feel that in such options the value of system as a tool of standardization is eroded. Some optional numbers are enclosed within parenthesis, i.e., round bracket.

For instance, at (848.99) (vol. 3; p. 814) French language literatures not requiring local emphasis, one finds a note that the use of this number is optional for libraries. Under such notes the official preference (i.e., the class number used by the Dewey Section of the LC) is also given. For example, after the instruction under (848.99), the official preference i.e. "Prefer 840 for all French language literatures," has also been indicated.

5. Centered headings

Sometimes a subject instead of being assigned a single class number is spread over a span of numbers, the two terminal numbers being connected by a hyphen. These centered headings or entries may occur at the section level or at its subdivisions. These are always given in the centre of the page, and on the left margin a chevron > sign indicates a centered heading.

For example :

>	383-388	Communications and transportation
>	384.1-384.6	Telecommunication

It is a clear breakdown of hierarchy, but permits larger space for expanding the number. In such entries a single class number is always indicated for comprehensive works on the topic. Under 384.1-384.6, one reads the instruction "Class comprehensive works in 384". Hence the proper class number for general works on telecommunication is 384. The device of centered headings is useful for the hospitality and brevity of notation.*

Hook number entries

Some numbers in the hierarchy of sub-divisions have no specific meaning -- a concise heading which could specifically mean a subject. Instead it is a sort of a peg on which many other named classes are hooked or hanged there. These numbers have headings such as "Miscellaneous..," "Others...", or "Specific...". In Ranganathan's Colon Classification such numbers are called quasi isolates. In chain indexing such links give out unsought headings. For example :

265.9	Other acts [Christian rites]
265.92	Consecrations and dedications
265.94	Exorcism

The first is a hook number which has only vague meaning. The other two specific numbers are hooked on it. However, this type of entry is of no practical consequences to the classifiers.

Notes

The schedules and tables comprise of entries. Each entry apart, from number/ notation and its corresponding verbal heading in natural language (showing hierarchy by indentions) contains many types of illustrated notes and instructions to guide a classifier. These various types of notes help the classifier in intended interpretation of the heading regarding what it should contain and what not. The ultimate aim is to achieve uniformity and consistency in applying the DDC system. There are in all 17 kinds of notes divided into four categories :

A. **Scope and Content Notes:** These includes definition, and what should be classed under that number.

1. **Definition notes :** Such a note gives a brief but dear definition of the class. Only a few entries contain such note, e.g., see at 139 Phrenology.
2. **Scope notes :** Such notes enumerate the boundaries of the class, e.g., 516.34 Analytic trigonometry or 541 Physical Chemistry. The purpose of both kinds of these notes is the same, i.e., to bring to surface the subsumed subtopics of a subject and to, demarcate the boundaries of that class.
3. **Number built notes :** Some number are found synthesised in the schedule, which otherwise the classifier could have done by following instructions. In such cases how of the synthesised number is given.

   In addition there are also some more readymade numbers in the schedules especially the ten main classes synthesised with standard subdivisions. e.g., 603 Dictionaries, etc. of Technology.
4. **Former-heading notes :** In some cases, the number, its contents and meanings remain the same but its verbal heading is changed to be in tune with current terminology. In such cases the previous heading in given With the note. "Former heading:...".

5. **Variant-name notes :** Synonymous terms are given in such notes, and these terms are also included in the relative index, e.g. 146.4 Positivism.

6. **Class-here notes :** Under many a class number, there are enumerated topic(s) with the instruction "Class here...". Such topics in fact being generally broader than the class number (or overlaps other numbers), and only for convenience are to be placed there. For example, under 343.08 Regulation of trade (Commerce), besides inclusion note one reads the instruction : "Class here commodity exchanges and exchange transactions". The tenor of such notes is clear. The topics mentioned in class-here notes may have standard subdivisions added to them.

   It also includes the note to class interdisciplinary and comprehensive works there.

B. **Inclusion notes :** These types of notes indicate some additional subtopics which are to be classed under that heading.

7. **Including notes :** Some subtopics are a part of a given number, may be temporarily. These are placed with the broader number only because they do not yet possess their own number. They are given a standing room. For example, 513.211 Addition, contains the note: "Including counting...". It means that counting is not essentially a part of Addition, and yet it does not have a separate number of its own. Hence such a subject has been given a standing room till it gets its own number. **No standard subdivision is to be added to such class numbers.**

   Some entries, especially in case of Taxonomy 570-590, have two including notes.

C. **Cross Reference Notes :** These notes refer in part or whole to some other number.

8. **Class-elsewhere notes :** These are in direct contrast to class-here notes. When a topic seemingly forming a part of a class belongs elsewhere, a note is given in the form : "Class... in...". For example, 181.12 Philosophy of Japan contains a note "Class Shinto philosophy in 181.09561". This also includes related note "Class comprehensive works in .... " and "class interdisciplinary works in ...."

9. **See references :** When a seemingly part of a class is given an independent number then the classifiers are directed to that number. It begins with "For..... see", e.g. in 191 Philosophy of US and Canada, we find a note *"For Middle American and Mexican philosophy, see 199.72"* [Italics original].

10. **See also references :** Obviously it refers to a related independent number for a comprehensive search, e.g.

676.2845	Vulcanized and parchment papers *See also 685 for parchment prepared from the skin of an animal.*

[Original italics]

Such references are given on reciprocal basis, as similar note under 685 refers to 676.2845.

In a classified catalogue See also references may be prepared under both the class numbers.

A *See also* note may also refer to more than one class, e.g., see under 153 Conscious mental processes and intelligence.

11. **See manual notes :** Entries in the schedules and tables are frequently linked with the manual in volume 1 of the DDC 23. This is not any cross reference but a sort of scope note for the guidance of the classifier referring to similar or analogous subjects. In the DDC 22 most the See manual reference were converted to See also references in the schedules, thus size of the manual was reduced for simplicities. For example, at 305.9 Occupational and miscellaneous [social] groups, we find a reference "*See Manual at 305.9 vs. 305.5*"

    (See also : Scope notes, and See also reference note)

D. **Notes that explain change or irregularities :** Such notes are of historical nature especially to help classifiers who switch to new edition from the previous one. These are:

12. **Revision notes:** If in a new edition a class is partially or completely revised, so a revision note is given under that class.

13. **Discontinued notes:** Apart from some numbers given in square brackets which have no subject meaning, or numbers recently discontinued are given in square brackets. Such discontinued numbers are invariably accompanied by a class-elsewhere note indicating the new number for that subject. For example, 343 [09942] Telegraph law Number discontinued class in 343.0994. It clearly means that this specific number has been merged with its broader class 343.0994 Telecommunication. Its purpose is to mark changes between two successive editions to help classifiers to switch from old to the new edition.

Such numbers are listed in the Section "Relocations and Discontinuations" (vol.1,pp.763-778).

14. **Relocation notes :** When in a new edition, as a result of relocation a subject, partially or wholly gets a different number, its previous number is also given at the new place. The former class number is enclosed within square brackets with a prefix "[*formerly...*]". For example, 459.982 Sardinian [language] [*formerly* 457.9] (*Italics original*). But when a number is partially relocated then the newly independent number is also given indicating its previous place with a note [*formerly also...*] It is a brief history of the classification of this topic in the DDC related to this revision.

15. **Do-not-use notes :** This kind of instruction is used when a regular place of a standard subdivision is shifted wholly or partially to some other number. If a number is wholly shifted then such a number is enclosed in square brackets. Such entries begin with a caveat "Do not use; class in..." e.g.,

    362 [.09] History, geographic treatment, biography[of social problems].

    Do not use; class in 362.9

    If it applies to a partial number then the number is not enclosed in square brackets, e.g.,

    069.028 Maintenance and repair[Muselogy].

    Do not use for maintenance and repair of museum objects; class in 069.53

16. **See Manual notes :** Manual now integral to volume 1 (pp 1-175) has become vital part of the DDC system for its use of correct and officially intended meaning of classes and notes in the schedules and tables. But it is only to be referred

occasionally than read as a whole. Therefore, in the schedules and tables the classifiers are frequently referred to the relevant sections of the manual which is arranged in T1/T6; 001-999 order. This note too often appears in the form "*See Manual at...*".

17. Standard Subdivisions are added ... notes

A new type of note clarifying explicitly the addition of a standard subdivision to a class number was introduced in the DDC-21(1996). It usually appears under a class number with a compound heading and explains to which part the standard subdivision, if needed, is to be added. For example:

636.73 Working and herding dogs.

Standard subdivisions are added for working and herding dogs together, for working dogs alone.

It is implied from this note that standard subdivision cannot be added to 636.73. Herding dogs. Probably herding dogs will get individual number in some future edition.

Number Building Notes or Instructions

This sort of note is central to the grammar of the DDC and forms the backbone of the synthetic apparatus in the system. Almost every class number in the DDC can be further extended whether there are immediate instructions or not. For example, the Standard Subdivisions of Table 1 may be added to any class number. In addition to such intrinsic provisions to many class numbers are appended "Add..." notes which may further be subdivided into two kinds:

1. Instructions specific to a number

Under many a class number are provided instructions extending a basic number with some other number or part thereof of a class number existing elsewhere in the schedules or tables. For example, under 547.1 "Physical and theoretical chemistry" is given the instructions" Add to base number 547.1 the numbers following 541 in 541.2–541.3". Such instructions are usually illustrated with at least one example.

2. Instructions common for a series of numbers

Sometimes a series of cognate class numbers are further extendable by another number. Instead of providing individual instructions, for convenience and simplicity, as well as for brevity of the schedules, instructions are provided at one place, while the headings of the class numbers to which such instructions apply are marked with an asterisk. Then at the foot of the page a footnote is given the meaning of the asterisk. For example:

547.4	*Aliphatic compounds
547.41	* Hydrocarbon
547.411	* Paraffins (Alkanes)
547.412	* Olefins (Alkenes)
547.413	* Acetylenes (Alkynes)

In the footnote on the same page is given the instruction:

"Add as instructed under 547". On going to class 547 one reads the detailed instructions : "Add to notation for each term identified by as follows :

04	Special topics
044	Theoretical chemistry
045	Physical chemistry
046	Analytical chemistry

We can synthesis a large variety of class numbers with such provision. For example :

Theoretical chemistry of hydrocarbons

547.41 + 044 = 547.41044

Analytical chemistry of hydrocarbons

547.41 + 046 = 547.41046

A related type of example is given therein at 328.4-.9 (p.415,vol.2) where all the numbers can be extended by a special table 01—092given there in ,e.g. Debates in Indian Parliament 328.54+02(debates)=328.5402

Such instructions have provided a citation order of the various facets and have increased number building power of the DDC.

Instructions to add from Tables 2-6

Under various entries there are explicit instructions to add from any of the Tables 2 to 6 ,whereas notations from Table 1can be added to almost any class number without instructions

In addition, there are instructions under many a class number to add from any of the six tables.

All these and other instructions must be carefully followed and implemented to build a correct class number.

Dot and spaces

It is generally forgotten that all the numerals used in DDC behave like decimal fractions. The decimal point has not been put in the beginning: it is supposed to be hidden there. But when a number gets lengthened beyond three basic digits a dot is inserted between the third and the fourth digit. This dot is only a pause and must not be misunderstood as the decimal point. Mathematically a decimal point occurs once in any numerical figure. Dot has no purpose except to break the monotony of numerals. For the same purpose, if a class number extends beyond six digits a space is left between the sixth and the seventh digit, and again between the ninth and the tenth digit, and so on. On this pattern, a space is left after every three digits coming after the dot. For example, the class number for "Super gravity" is transcribed as

530.142 3. Similarly the class number for Thyristors is transcribed as 621.381 528 7. These spaces and dot give relief to the eyes and facilitate short while retention of the class number in the memory – during the passage from the catalogue to the stacks. However spaces are not given when a number is assigned to an item.

2

How to Assign and Build Class Numbers in the DDC

Hold book in ryt hand and turn with left, then both class numbers and index heds show most plainly on left marjins and reference is quicker when eye follows left pages only. —*Melvil Dewey*

The work of practical classification consists of two phases: intellectual work in sorting out the specific subject of the document under classification; and the craft of assigning the appropriate notations to the ascertained specific subject. Yes! It is a craft, an art learned over time. These two phases are respectively termed as:

(a) Subject analysis

(b) Locating class number and number building

These two phases can be likened to medical diagnosis and prescription, respectively. If the ailment is correctly diagnosed, then prescription for its cure can safely be entrusted to skilled hands. The former is intellectual work, and for that reason the more important of the two. It is indeed the essence of classifying and somewhat independent of the classification system used. Determination of the specific subject of a given document is a cognitive art. It is no exaggeration to say that it requires intuitive insight. It only comes through a wide acquaintance with the topic and the literature upon it. Such knowledge may constantly improve through one's life, though it may never reach perfection. Indeed, widely read persons have more flair than others in determining the specific subject of a book. Intense specialization and rapidly advancing frontiers of knowledge have, nevertheless, made it more difficult, if not impossible, to know everything about every subject.

The specific subject of a document may be determined by examining the document under classification through its title, sub-title, preface, blurb, table of contents, and the text itself; the name of the author, subject index, and the cited references may also provide some valuable clues. A classifier may occasionally consult some reference tools for help in this task. If all these efforts fail, the last resort is to consult some subject expert. This so far is the work in the domain of knowledge classification. Besides determining the specific subject of a book, there may arise many difficulties to class especially a composite book at its appropriate place. For all such difficulties one can surely count on the classic book of W.S. Merrill: *Code for Classifiers: Principles Governing the Consistent Placing of Books in a System of Classification.* (Chicago: A.L.A., 1939). The code is independent of any classification system.

A librarian is concerned with book classification, as distinguished from the work of knowledge classification. Therefore, for book classification, besides the knowledge of knowledge qua knowledge, one needs to know the structure of knowledge, its subdivisions and various adjuncts in a particular system of classification. Library Classification is the work of match making: fitting the subject into an already created place in the schedules. A classifier is essentially a match-maker. To do this is needed the schedules and the technique to operate it. Contrary to Ranganathan's views, the work of a classifier is more a matter of flair than anything else. Once the specific subject has been determined, there is further need to determine the field of study in which it falls, and the way of treatment by the author in context of the classification system used: that is, determine from what view the subject has been treated. For example, a subject, say Economics, may be treated from the viewpoint of its philosophy, theory, history, research or from the practical application viewpoint. Further the above document treated from any viewpoint may be a dictionary, a journal or a mere collection of data in tabulated form. Not only this, any of the above internal or external arrangements may reach us in any of the numerous physical media, namely a book, microfiche, video cassette, a film, or a CD-ROM, or an WWW item. Thus a classifier has to sort out four different aspects of a given document.

(1) topic
(2) discipline
(3) point of view
(4) form

After this is done, the only task left is to codify the subject and its treatment of viewpoint into the decimal notation.

To enter the Decimal Classification the better way is through its structured ladder. The other way is through the Index. One must know at the outset (through knowledge of the scheme) to what Main class, and then to what Division and finally to what Section of the DDC the given work pertains.

For efficiency, it is better to commit to memory the 100 Divisions of the scheme. It is not absolutely necessary, though surely lessens the avoidable leafing through the DDC schedules to assign a class number. With experience, many Sections come on one's fingertips. In this way, we go on narrowing our approach successively at each step. Many a time we reach the section concerned through our personal knowledge of the scheme bypassing the scanning of the Ten Main classes and the Divisions. If a subject is concerned with, say, education, we will go to 370 in the Schedules; and if it is concerned with medicine we look at 610 in the Schedules. Even if one is not conversant with the Divisions, this part of the class number should be worked through via the Three Summaries (given on pages v-xvi, volume 2) of the DDC. The real need to consult the Schedules arises on arriving at the correct section. To carry the search for the appropriate and specific class number all the immediate divisions of a section, viz, subsections are further scanned, which, for the convenience of the classifiers, are usually given at one place. Many summaries and multilevel summaries have been given at the beginning of many densely detailed classes. For example, see the two-level summary of the class 570 Biology on pages 1126-1127, Vol. 2. Such summaries which are numerous are helpful to locate the desired section and subsection at one glance only. Such summaries are just like the map of a multistoried building given at the entrance. These summaries have a great reference value, and save the time and patience of the classifier in nabbing the desired class number. Multilevel summaries, a new feature since the DDC-20 are of great help in this work. These summaries also save the print schedules from physical wear and tear as the classifiers do less flipping of pages.

A classifier is like a traveller who has to select her path at every crossing -where many roads diverge in various directions. By choosing the right direction at every crossing the classifier does not have to trudge through the whole text to reach the desired class number. In this way the even buried numbers may be traced. The Number selected may be the desired specific number, or one that may act as the base number to build further the coextensive class number matching exactly the subject of the document under classification. The further extension of the class number may be either from the auxiliary Tables or the Schedules. (This is discussed in the appropriate chapters).

To illustrate this, say our subject is "Money". At the first instance we need to examine whether the core subject of the book is "Minting of money" or "Economics of money". If the latter is the case, a knowledgeable DDC practitioner will tell at the outset that it is a subject of social sciences, that is, of economics. On going to 330 Economics in the third summary (Volume 2, p.x) we see that it pertains to 332 Financial economics. At this stage, we shift to the schedules proper at class number 332 (volume 2, p. 450). Examining the summary of subsections of 332 (Volume 2, p.450) we find the subsection 332.4 Money matches squarely with the subject of the given document. Now we will shift to the subsection 332.4 (p. 456, vol. 2) and scan its sub-subsections. We see here that the number 332.4 is quite appropriate. By assigning the class number 332.4 to the document our search for the appropriate and specific class number ends.

Take one more example: Anatomy of Human Lungs. The book deals with a human body organ, so in a twinkling, an experienced classifier can tell that it belongs to the main class applied sciences, and then to its division medicine, which deals with the human body, its parts, and functions. Looking through the Division 610 Medicine, we find that Anatomy (the science of human organs) is 611, which is the desired Section. At this stage we shift our search to the Schedules at 611 (Vol. 3, p.15). Looking through the summary of the subsections of 611 (on page 14 we find that 611.2 Respiratory organs is the next appropriate choice. Examining the further divisions (subsections) of 611.2 (page 18) we find Lungs enumerated at 611.24, which is our specific number.

If the subject is the Study and teaching of lungs anatomy, the Dewey classifier, will know that study and teaching is an auxiliary aspect of the core subject Lungs anatomy, and the notation for the auxiliary aspect is to be taken from Table 1: Standard subdivisions. Both notations are to be combined as per the rules.

In the Introduction the number building process has been described as a four-way technique:

1. Determine the various facets of the publication
2. Determine which facets can be indicated through the notation. If all the facets cannot be included, then follow the order of precedence to select the facets for inclusion
3. Arrange the facets in the proper order. It is called Citation of facets. Citation order is always clearly explained in the number-building instructions. One has only to find the right base
4. Follow the add instructions.

If we add here the first step as determining the subject and discipline to which it belongs then it becomes the general procedure for all sorts of number building procedures.

In fact, this is too facile a view of the process of assigning a class number to a subject. In reality, a classifier may encounter many unanticipated difficulties. Firstly, it may be borne in mind that we assign class numbers not to the title but to the specific subject of the document under classification. If the title is a fanciful one and the subject has not been explained in the subtitle, the specific subject of the book must be determined from the text. For example, a book with the title "Asian Drama" could be a book of creative literature, but is a work on the economic development of the

Third World. Sometimes the title may look incomplete. For example, a book may have a title "Shakespeare". At the outset one may not know whether it is the biography of William Shakespeare, or his evaluation as dramatist, or poet, or merely a collection of his works. To classify correctly one will have to supply the wanting words in the title from other parts of the text. On the other hand, there may be many superfluous words in a title. In such cases the title must be stripped of such meaningless but decorative words, and the class number be assigned only to the core words connoting the subject succinctly. For example, a book may have the title "A Long and Exciting Expedition to the Himalayas". Here Himalayan expedition is the core subject, and for the purpose of classifying one will have to ignore the remaining words, however perceptibly important these may be to the author. Melvil Dewey's introduction to the 12th edition of the DDC is still valuable in this context. Ranganathan's eight steps for classifying a document may be of great help to a novice classifier.

A difficulty in classifying may ensue from the fact that though no word in the title is redundant, yet it may not be possible to assign a co-extensive class number to the whole of the title. Take the title "Classification in School Libraries". In the DDC the class number for classification is 025.42 and that for school libraries is 027.8. There is no provision to integrate these two numbers. Here we will have to make a choice between the two numbers. Editors usually advise us to choose the more concrete of the two, which usually comes later in the schedules. Many a time, the order of precedence is given: as under 362 Social welfare problems and services at 363.1, and 364. A table of precedence is also given for Standard Subdivisions in Table 1. Choice may also depend upon the author's emphasis, or the needs of an individual library.

Similarly, a book may treat more than one subject at

a time. The classifier will have to choose a generic class number if possible or give a class number for one of the subjects and ignore the others. The reason is that the DDC still aims to group documents broadly as contrasted from the faceteers ambition to make classification an artificial language of notation translating equivalently the subject of the book into the notation used. DDC does not aim to provide a unique class number for every document in the library. Only Call number does it.

Still another difficulty may lie for the new subjects yet not listed in the schedules. In such cases the book may be assigned to the closest possible broader class number, which may broadly cover the subject of the book. In such cases, the auxiliary tables are not added to the class number, even if the subject specially demands this. It is not done because the new edition may probably provide a specific class number by just adding a digit or two to the previous number; and the number from auxiliary tables may be added then. For example, "Teaching computers in elementary schools" was classed in 372.35 in DDC-20, as there was no separate number for computers in schools. Therefore no subdivision could be added then to that number. In the DDC-21 Computer teaching was given a separate number, viz., 372.34. Now in the DDC-23 instructions have been made more explicit as to where the subdivisions are to be added or avoided. For example, see the following entry:

372.35 Science and technology

Subdivisions are added for science and technology together, for science alone.

For mathematics, see 372.7

It means that teaching of technology in elementary schools though placed at 372.35 will not admit further divisions. Probably in the next edition there could be a separate number for teaching of technology. For such problems the editors have provided guidance in DDC-23 Volume 1, Sec. 8.8 (p. lx).

Another important problem is the interpretation of schedules as to the intended official meaning. In spite of many notes, and cross references, it is still an elusive task. Subjectivity in interpretation can never be ruled out; and subject analysts may disagree among themselves on the connotations of a heading and on the question of assigning a correct class number to a given book. J.B. Friis-Hansen aptly says that "identical use of DC in all countries is impossible and hardly any chance of it exists. Identical classification of the same book is a difficulty in one country, even by one person on different weekdays". Centralised cataloguing systems such as CIP data," MARC records, WorldCat of OCLC, various national and trade bibliographies using the DDC help to lesson this inevitable problem to an uncertain extent. Purpose of the Manual in volume 1 is to promote uniformity in interpretation by different classifiers. The it is a boon for the practical classifiers in the library for uniformity and consistency.

3

Practical Number Building

Synthesis through "Add to ....." instructions from the schedules:

1. Add to from 001 to 999
2. Add to a class number from some other small portion of the schedules.
3. Add to from the same Division/ Section.
4. Add to through special provision (facet indicator) including the 04 General special:
5. Add from any internal table given for that class
6. Add from any of the six tables in volume 1.

Most of the specific subjects have readymade class numbers in the schedules as the DDC is basically an enumerative scheme. For some others especially multifaceted subjects the number will have to be built on a given base number. The choice of the base number is the most important step to build the desired number. S.R. Ranganathan's PMEST facet formula is of much help in such matters, but that is no substitute to the familiarity with the DDC Schedules.

On arriving at a specific number, it may be seen, that

if required, the number may be further subdivided by some number or its part as taken from the Schedules or Tables. Broadly, the above kind of additions may be divided into six categories (1-6 as above). One should, however, be careful not to build a class number which is otherwise already enumerated in the Schedules. Nor one can join two class numbers in the schedules without instructions. One general piece of advice is that the decimal point should only be put after the first three digits when the whole number has been built.

(1) Addition of any Number from the whole Schedules 001-999 to any given Base Number

One is merely required to add another whole number to a given base number from the schedules. It is as easy as that.

025.46 is Library classification of specific disciplines and subjects. For library classification of any discipline one find the instruction to add notation 001-999 to the base number 025.46. It means we are to add the class number from the schedule of that subject to the base class number 025.46, e.g., Classification of books on Mathematical analysis:

025.46 + 515 = 025.46515

(515 is the class number for Mathematical analysis)

Similarly, "Library Classification of Indian Philosophy" gets the class number:

025.46+181.4= 025.461814

Similarly, 026 Libraries, archives, information centres devoted to specific subjects and disciplines is to be further subdivided like 001-999 for the class number of a library devoted to any specific subject:

Science Libraries

026+500=026.5

Terminal (or filler) zeroes are redundant in a decimal fraction; these are dropped in the ultimate class number:

Libraries of library and information science

026 + 020 = 026.02

Libraries devoted to Indian philosophy

026 + 181.4 = 026.1814

Libraries on inorganic chemistry

026 + 546 = 026.546

Similarly,

Science journalism

070.499 + 500 = 070.4495

Sports journalism

070.449 + 790 = 070.44979

331.124 Job vacancies, (Job Openings),

331.1241 In industries and occupations other than extractive, manufacturing, construction.

For job opportunities in the Military service: to the designated base 331.1241, as per instructions, we are to add the class number of Military science taken from the schedules:

331.1241 + 355 = 331.1241355

Job opportunities in library and information science

331.1241+ 020 = 331.124102

Aptitude tests for ability in mathematics

153.94 Aptitude tests

153.94001-.94999 Tests for aptitudes in specific fields

= 153.94 + 510 (Math) 153.9451

Aptitude test in Music

153.94 + 780 (Music) = 153.9478

Library acquisition of reading materials in sciences

025.27 + 500 = 025.275

Acquisition of books in libraries on Indian history

025.27 + 954 = 025.27954

Women librarians : A Social Study

305.43 + 02 (from 020) = 305.4302

Many more such examples can be enlisted of topics admitting further division by the whole range of the Schedules. **However, this device is not to be used of its is own: Classifiers should use this number building device only on invitation, though one may be tempted to use such methods on one's own initiative.**

It is quite obvious that whenever a class number admits further division from 001-999, standard subdivisions, if required for that subject, are added with three zeroes, as two zeroes may be used sometimes for a subject class number. In such cases instructions exist for addition of a standard subdivision with the required number of zeroes:

Journal of curriculum

375.0005

Similarly,

History of special libraries devoted to various specific disciplines:

026.0009

Archives: An international journal

026.0005

(2) Add to a designated Base a portion of the Class Number from some smaller area of the Schedules.

Instead of admitting any whole class number from anywhere in the Schedules, a designated base may require addition from some specific part of the Schedules, from a single main class, or division or a section or even smaller than that. It is a specialised extension of the instructions Add to from 001-999. In such cases, instead of adding the whole class number to the specified base number, a portion of a number is added. Here the common digits from a series of class numbers are removed, and the digits following the generic digits are added to the designated base number. This makes the resulting class number brief, without any ambiguity in the series of the class number that such instructions yield. There will be no difficulty in the retranslation of the class number into ordinary language, too. For example:

181	Oriental philosophy
181.04-.09	[Oriental Philosophy] based on specific religions.

To derive the class number for any specified religious philosophy, we are instructed under 181.04-.09 to add the number following 29 in 294-299 to the base number 181.0 (vol. 2, p. 160). For example:

Buddhist philosophy

The number for Buddhism is 294.3

Here the digits after 29 are "43". These are to be added to 181.0. The derived number thus is:

181.0+43 = 181.043

Similarly

Confucian Religion has the class number:

299.512

So Confucian philosophy will get the class number:

181.0+9512=181.09512

Let us take another example:

331.2	Compensation and other conditions of employment
331.204	In specific industries...

331.2042—.2049 In extractive, manufacturing, construction industries and occupations

For a class number for wages/conditions of working in any specified industry related to manufacturing, extraction, or instruction, we are required to add to the base number 331.204 the numbers following 6 in 620-690:

Wages of agricultural labour

The number for Agriculture is 630 and the digits which follow 6 are 30 to be added to the base number 331.204

Hence;

331.204 + 30 = 331.2043

Working conditions for miners

331.204 + 22 (from 622) = 331.20422

(The class number for mining being 622)

Demand for carpenters

331.123 + 94 (from 694 carpenters) =331.12394

Physiology of Mammals

Animal Physiology

571.1

Here we are asked to add to 571.1 the number following 59 in 591-599. The class number for mammals is 599. Hence the number is:

571.1 + 9 (from 599) = 571.19

Physiology of Primates

571.1 + 98 (from 599.8 Primates) = 571.198

Some more examples:

Guides to a Christian life for members of specific denominations and sects

248.48

For specific sects, we are to add to the above base (248.48)

the numbers following 28 in 281 - 289, e.g.:

Guides to a Puritan life

248.48 + 59 (from 285.9) = 248.4859

Guides for Methodists

248.48 + 7 (from 287) = 248.487(Methodist is 287)

Wheat trade

381.4 [Trade in] Specific products and services

381.41 Product of Agriculture

381.413-.418 Specific products [of Agriculture]

Here we are instructed to add to the base 381.41 the number following 63 in 633-638.

For wheat the number is 63 in 633—638

For wheat the number is 633.11. Hence we will add 311 to the above designated base

381.41 + 311 (from 633.11) = 381.41311

Reviews of documents in microforms

028.13+6 (from 011.36) = 028.136

Reviews of Braille books

028.16 + 3 (from 011.63) = 028.163

(3) "Add to..." From the same Division

There is a subtle difference between an "add to..." instruction from the same Division/ Section, and the number being added from some remote part of the Schedules. The difference lies not in the method, but in the nature of the part of the number added. As said earlier, a Division is subdivided into Sections: second Section and its sub-divisions enumerate the action facet, while the rest of the Sections enumerate the personality facet, to speak in the Ranganathan language. These personality facets from sections XX3-XX9* are further divisible by the facets of XX1 or XX2; thereby giving the general citation order as personality followed by action. Actually it is addition of a secondary facet to a primary facet. One can say that this technique has made the scheme faceted. Take the example:

Cotton harvesting

Here cotton is the concrete subject, therefore it will form the base number. Obviously, this is a subject of agriculture; going to 630 Agriculture we find the number for Cotton at 633.51.

It is marked with an asterisk i.e.,* which at the footnote explains: "Add as instructed under 633-635". Going back to the instructions given at page 307 (vol. 3) we find a series of instructions. The very first instruction is relevant to our purpose. We are asked to add to the base (class) number the digits following 631.5 in 631.51-631.56. The class number for Harvesting is 631.55. It means that as per instructions, we are to add to 633.51 the numbers following 631.5, i.e., 5 only. Therefore, the complete class number for Cotton harvesting is

633.51 + 5 = 633.515

Similarly

Soil preparation for cotton

633.51+1=633.511

Cotton seeds

633.51 + 21 (from 631.521) = 633.5121

New varieties of cotton

633.51 + 23 = 633.5123

Cotton yield

633.51 + 58 = 633.5158

Cotton storing

633.51 + 68 (from 631.568) = 633.5168

Take another example:

Evolution in Porifera

Here Porifera (sponges) with the class number 593.4 will form the base number. Here we are told to add as instructed under 592-599 (p. 1228, vol.2). The instruction relevant to our purpose is 1 General topics of natural history. First we are to add 1 to the designated base number and further add the number following 591 in 591.3-591.7. In 591 the number for evolution is 591.38. Therefore, we are to add only 38 to the above compound number :

593.4 + 1 + 38 (from 591.38) = 593.4138

(Here 1 acts as a facet indicator. **The general principle that emerges is that we can add all the subdivisions of 591.3-591.7 to all the class numbers from 592-599 through a facet indicator 1.)**

Let us now find the class number for

Physical adaptation of Invertebrates.

Invertebrates 592*

Asterisk instructs us to add 1 for natural history of invertebrates and then to the base we are to add the numbers following 591 in 591.3-591.7. The class number for "Physical adaptation" is 591.4.

Thus we are required to add 4 to 592+1. The complete class, number, therefore, is :

592.1 + 4 (from 591.4) = 592.14

Similarly:

Physiology of Invertebrates

Physiology of Animals 571.1

571.1 + 2 (from 592) = 571.12

Evolution of Invertebrates

592 + 1 + 38 (from 591.38) = 592.138

Anatomy of Invertebrates

571.3+1 (as under 591 - 592) + 2 (from 592)
571.312

Ecology of Invertebrates

592 + 1 (from 592 - 599) + 7 (from 591.7) = 592.17

Similarly in 294.4 Jainism, specific aspects of Jainism have been placed at 294.41—294.48. These aspects can be individualised as in 201—209. For this we are told by the footnote to add to the base 294.4 as instructed under 290 (p. 290, vol. 2). For specific aspects we are to add 1-9 from 201-209. Let us take an example of the Sacred Books of Jains. Our base number is 294.4 and the number for sacred books in 201-209 is 208.2. Thus to the base 294.4, we will add 82. Hence the class number for the Sacred books of Jains is

294.4 + 82 (from 208.2) = 294.482

Similarly:

Jain eschatology

294.4 + 23 (from 202.3) =294.423

Sacred places of Jains

294.4 + 35 (from 203.5) =294.435

Worship in Jainism

294.4 + 43 (from 204.3) = 294.443

Jain saints

294.4 + 213 (from 202.13) = 294.4213

Problems in acquisition of government publications

025.28 + 34 (from 025.3434) = 025.2834.

Collection development in Elementary school libraries

025.218 + 78222 (from 027.8222) = 025.21878222

Book selection in national libraries

025.218 + 75 (from 027.5) = 025.21875*

Reference service in children libraries

025.527 + 7625 (from 027.625) = 025.5277625

4-5 Add to... through a Facet Indicator

Sometimes some special subdivisions applicable to a series of numbers of a Section are enumerated in the beginning of the same section. These internal tables of special facets are of general applicability within the same section. Instructions are provided against each subsection and their further divisions for adding the desired facet.

Prevention of heart diseases

616.12 + 05 (p. 87, vol. 3) = 616.1205*

Case histories of heart diseases

616.12 + 09 (p. 88, vol. 3) = 616.1209

Similar instructions are also found under the subdivisions of 618

618.1	Gynecology
618.11	Diseases of the ovaries

As per similar instructions one can add to this number any required facet enumerated under the heading 618.1-618.8 (pp. 154-156, vol.3)

Preventive measures for ovary diseases

618.11 +052=618.11052

Laser Surgery treatment for ovary diseases

618.11 + 0598 (p. 156, vol.3) = 618.110598

Take an example from 746 Textile arts. To many of the subdivisions of 746 may be added special subdivisions given under 746 (p. 613, vol.3); and whenever these special facets are admissible such places have been marked with an asterisk*

For instance, for a work on Crochet patterns, we find that specific class number for Crocheting is 746.434 and as per instruction we add to it the number for pattern given on page 613 (vol.3). Thus the complete class number is:

746.434 + 041 = 746.434041

Pattern in woven rugs

746.72 + 041 = 746.72041

Take an example in 546 Inorganic chemistry. Here almost all the individual elements are extendable by some special subdivisions enumerated once for all in the beginning under the general heading 546 Inorganic chemistry (p. 1066, vol. 2). The instruction here is to add to each subdivision identified by* as follows:

1 The element

2 Compounds

22 Acids and bases,

24 Salts

25 Complex compounds

....

5 Physical chemistry

6 Analytical chemistry

For example, if the subject is Potassium salts, the class number for Potassium chemistry is 546.383:

Salt is a special facet having the number 24.

The complete class number for Potassium salts is

546.383 + 24 = 546.38324

Similarly, the special facet number for the physical chemistry of individual elements is 5. As per instruction, it is further divisible as the subdivisions of 541.3 as in 541.33-541.39. We are to add to 5 the digits following 541.3 in 541.33-541.39.

For example:

Physical chemistry of potassium

546.383 +5= 546.3835

Chemical reaction kinetics of potassium (a topic of

physical chemistry)

The base number is 546.383. Since it is the physical chemistry aspect, we add 5

546.383 + 5 = 546.3835

The digit 5 is further extendable by the subdivisions of 541.3. The class number for chemical reaction kinetics is 541.394

Here the digits that follow 541.3 are 94. Hence the complete class number for chemical kinetics of potassium is

546.383 + 5 + 94 (from 541.394) = 546.383594

Similarly:

Isotopes of potassium

546.383+5+ 88 (from 541.388 Isotopes) = 546.383588

Photochemistry of potassium

546.383+5+5(from 541.35 Photochemistry) = 546.38355

Analytical chemistry of sodium

546.382+6 (Analytical chemistry, p.1066 vol.2)

546.3826

Some of the facets applicable to some of the subdivisions of 721-729: Specific aspects of architecture have been enumerated thereunder on p. 555 Volume 3.

722 Architecture from earliest times to ca.300

722.11 Ancient Chinese architecture

As per instruction, it admits the facets enumerated under 721-729:

Drawings of ancient Chinese architecture

722.11 + 0222 = 722.110222

Architectural remodeling of theatre buildings

725.822 + 0286 = 725.8220286

Architecture of buildings for the physically handicapped: An Encyclopedia

725.54+03=725.5403.

6. Add from any of the Six Tables

See chapters 5-10 of this book.

4

Order of Precedence

Notwithstanding the many synthetic devices in the DDC, sometimes we are not able to provide a co-extensive class number for a given complex subject having many facets. Theoretically, such facets are combinable but the DDC does not allow them to unite in a single class number. Inevitably in such cases some facets will have to be ignored. The problem arises in deciding which facet to choose, and which facet to ignore. As a general rule, more specific facets are preferred over the less specific facets. But this measure of specificity is not left to the arbitration of a classifier. Under many class numbers or centered headings, the schedules provide a Precedence Table that determines the priorities of the two or more class numbers; gives clear direction as to which class number is to be chosen in case of choice between two or more class numbers.

In the Schedules, for example, under 155.42-155.45. Psychology of specific children by attributes (p. 139, vol. 2), is given the following table of precedence:

Exceptional children	155.45
Children by status and relationships	155.44
Children in specific age groups	155.42

Children by sex 155.43

For example, take the subject Psychology of Preschool girls. Girls and preschool children are different subdivisions of 155.4 Child psychology, and the schedule does not provide any instruction to combine them. The two possible class numbers are:

153.423 Preschool children

153.433 Girls

As per the table of precedence given above, 155.42 and its subdivisions are to be preferred over 155.43 Children by sex. Hence the correct class number for Psychology of Preschool girls is 155.423, not 155.433.

Similarly:

Psychology of gifted boys

155.45 + 5 = 155.455 (from 371.91-371.97 where gifted children is 371. 95)

Here as per the precedence table, we, ignored the sex facet and further elucidated the preferred number as per instructions under 155.45 Exceptional children. **This in fact is the number for Psychology of gifted children.**

Another table of precedence is given at 362 Social problems and welfare services (p.723, vol.2). Say, we have a book on:

Providing welfare service to poor women.

Welfare Services to Poor is 362.5.

Services to women is 362.83.

As per the table of precedence under 362 the number 362.83 is to be given precedence over 362.5. Hence the correct class number is 362.83.

Similarly:

Remedial Welfare services to old age alcoholics

362.2928, not 3626

Another precedence table can be found at 641.5 Cooking (p.359, vol 3).

Vegetarian cooking for travel

641. 5636, not 641. 575

Time saving cooking for armed forces

641.57, not 641.555

Cooking breakfast for South Asians

641.52, not 641.592+914 (Table 5)

Cooking lunch in schools

641.571, not 641.53

Another precedence order occurs at 649.1 Child rearing (p. 386, vol. 3)

Here instead of giving any priority table there is a simple instruction that of the two numbers, the number coming last in the schedules is to be preferred.

Rearing preschool girls

649.133, not 649.123

Home care for exceptional girls

649.15, and not 649.133

Rearing deaf boys

649.15+12 (dividing like 371.91-371.97)

=649.1512, not 649.132

Another table of precedence occurs at 657.1-657.9 Elements of accounting (p. 398, vol.3)

Auditing fixed assets

657.73, not 657.45

Public accounting for non-profit organisations.

657.98, not 657.61

Cost accounting in small hotels and restaurants

657.837 + 0 + 42 (dividing like 657.1-657.7 as per

instruction under 657.837)=657.837042, not 657.9042

Book keeping in nonprofit hospitals

657.8322+0+2 (Dividing like 657.1-657.7)

=657.832202, not 657.98

A small precedence table also occurs at 747.9 Specific interior decorations (p. 620, vol.3)

Interior decorative lighting for weddings

747.92, not 747.93

Interior decoration with houseplants for parties

747.98, not 747.93

At 757 Paintings of human figures and their parts, a precedence table is also given (p. 628, vol .3)

Paintings of nude women

757.4 and not 757.2

Miniature portraits of men

757.7 and not 757.3

When there are no instructions, a more specific class number is given precedence over a less specific number. **One mechanical formula to weigh the specificity of the two class numbers is: of the two class numbers one with a zero and the other having no zero, the latter is more specific, hence given precedence** (Rule 5.7 (E) p. xlix, vol. 1). For example:

Exchange rate of gold coins

332.456, not 332.4042

Political offences by the Mafia

364.131, not 364.106

Role of teachers in personal guidance programmes

371.46, not 371.4046

Team teaching in private schools

371.148 not 371.02

Wooden chairs and tables

684.13,not 684.104

Maintenance and repair of beds

684.15, not 684.1044

On the same principle, a class number with one zero will have precedence over a class number with two zeroes, and so on.

Sometimes the DDC replaces a table of precedence by a single instruction to choose an earlier or later notation (see Rule 9.6 p. lxv-lxvi, vol. 1). For example, at 331.3-331.6 Labour force by personal attributes we get the instruction (p. 438, vol. 2): "Unless other instructions are given, class complex subjects with aspects in two or more subdivisions of this schedule in the number coming first in the schedules..."

For example:

Labour by young women

331. 34, not 331. 4

Similarly a note could instruct us to choose the latter number as given under 305.9. Sociology of occupational and miscellaneous groups.

Sociology of unemployed doctors

305.961, not 305.906941

Sometimes the table of precedence is simply replaced by class elsewhere notes. For example, under 025 Operations of libraries, archives, information centers one reads the instruction: "Class comprehensive works on operations in specific kinds of institutions in 026-027". According to this instruction, we have for

Administration of school libraries

027.8, not 025.1

Classification in government libraries

027.5, not 025.42

But this formula does not apply to

025.2 Collection development and acquisition Book selection in specific types of institutions

025.218

Here one reads the instruction "Add to base number 025.218 the number following 02 in 026-027"

For example:

Book selection in school libraries

025.218 + 78 = 025.21878, not 027.8

Book selection in government libraries

025.218 + 75 =025.21875, not 027.5

Book selection in the Library of Congress (LC)

025.218+7573(for 027.573 LC) =025.2187573

The objective of the order of precedence tables, citation orders, and a host of notes, especially cross reference notes, class here or elsewhere notes is to avoid cross classification and to strike maximum uniformity and standardization in the application and interpretation of the Schedules and Tables. It enhances inter-indexer and intra-indexer consistency.

5

Use of Table 1: Standard Subdivisions

Information which is the predominant basis of library classification is an abstract entity. It cannot have any form by itself. It requires some physical medium for its capturing, dissemination, and preservation. A document which is a source of knowledge has always some physical form. Library classification deals with documents. Library classification, in effect, deals with information as recorded in documents. Therefore, library classification has to take into full account the outer and inner attributes of these physical objects embodying knowledge. It maybe described by the following equation:

Library Classification = Knowledge Classification + Viewpoint of the presentation of the text + Physical attributes of the document = Subjects + Internal form + External form.

These documentary forms are both internal and external. For example, it may be expedient in a library to separate a microfilm, or a CD-ROM, from a book, though the specific subject of these three may precisely be the same.

It is equally expedient to distinguish between a dictionary and a periodical of a subject; as well as the philosophical viewpoint from the historical one of the same subject. To account for such physical attributes of the documents, Melvil Dewey in the second edition of the scheme (1885) separated such non-subject forms of the documents and listed them in the beginning of each division. These tables can be added to any class number, and always remain the same in name and notation. **The notation for such recurring concepts always starts with a zero and has a meaning only when attached to some class; it cannot be used independently.** These are called "standard" because their meaning and notation remain the same wherever these are used.* What started truly as "form divisions" have evolved (with the complexities and varieties of incoming documents) to an agglomeration of some complex but recurring concepts termed as standard subdivisions. The standard subdivisions as they stand today in DDC23 (Volume 1, pp. 179-209) may broadly be categorized as under:

01 ; parts of 02, 07, and 09	Viewpoints
02 partially, 03, 05 and 06	Physical (Bibliographic) forms of the treatment of subjects
04, 08 and to some extent 09	Facet indicators to introduce a new facet

The scope of the standard subdivisions has been widened so much that it is advisable to go through Table 1 (in volume 1) to know their scope and variety. Knowledge of their nature and scope will surely add to the efficiency of classifiers. Rules for adding standard subdivisions to a class number have been provided in Sections 8.3 to 8.12 of the Introduction to the Dewey Decimal Classification in Volume 1 (p. lix-lxii). Here rules are given on how to use Table 1. Some brief instructions to apply them and the order of preference also precede the core Table 1. A great many instructions regarding standard subdivisions are found in the Manual on (pp. 5-17, vol. 1). Rules for adding an ss are summarised as follows:

1. A Standard subdivision is added to the ultimate schedule number of the document in question. Having reached the most specific class number, we do not necessarily need an invitation to add a standard subdivision from Table 1.

   Encyclopaedia of Islam

   297+03=297.03

   (Here Islam is the subject and encyclopaedia a standard subdivision).

   Encyclopedia of the Holy Koran

   297.12203

   History of the Ahmadiya movement

   297.86+09=297.8609

   (We have added ss 03 and 09; though there are no instructions to do so at these class numbers).

2. Subjects whose specific class numbers do not yet exist in the schedules should not be expanded with a standard subdivision.

   For example:

   Standards for goat's milk

Standards is an ss whose number is-0218 in Table 1. Goat's milk is a subject of animal husbandry. Milk production is 637.14 (which is cow's milk). All other kinds of milk are put under 637.17 with no further subdivision. Consequently, no specific class number has been provided for goat's milk. Therefore, as per the rules, we cannot add standard subdivisions here; the correct class number, therefore, is 637.17, and not 637.170218. This is done not because of any structural difficulty; it is an advice to ease expansion in future. May be some future edition provides a number for goat's milk, which probably would be a subdivision of 637.17. If now any ss is added to 637.17 it may entail total effacing and rewriting when we would provide co-extensive class number in conformity with some future edition. Moreover, to assign a standard subdivision to a number implies that the subdivision applies to the entire contents of the number; you mislead when you assign a standard subdivision to a part of a class.

3. Usually two standard subdivisions are not applied in succession to a class number. If a subject poses two standard subdivisions, then only one is to be applied on preferential basis, and the other is to be ignored. A table of preferences is prefixed to the Table 1. If we examine the preferential order, it becomes obvious that facet indicator General Special is followed by viewpoints, and the real form divisions come in the end. **It means internal forms are to be preferred over the external forms.** However, in Table 1- 093-099, there are provisions for adding standard subdivisions to standard subdivisions.

Let us take the example "Encyclopaedia of Organisations on Applied Psychology". Here encyclopaedia and organisation both are ss with the notations 03 and 06, respectively. Only one of them is to be added. As per the Precedence table, 06 is to be given preference over 03. Therefore, the correct class number is 158.06, not 158.03 or any number combining the two ss, viz., 158.0306

Similarly, a Directory of Library Schools in India will get the class number

020.71154 instead of 020.2554

Here ss-07 is preferred over 025

Therefore, whenever two standard subdivisions seem applicable to a work, this table may be consulted to know which of them is to be applied, and which is to be ignored, when all things are equal. When one standard subdivision concept is being stressed or is clearly more important, it is used, no matter what the preference table says.

Irregularities

At some places in the schedules the standard subdivision is already attached to a class number. Some of these are given a variant meaning to suit a local situation. Meanings of some of the ss are locally extended.

Extension in Meaning

If any of the ss when applied to a class gets some local name in that context, then in that schedule all such proper standard subdivisions are to be used. In all such cases, the notation is compatible with Table 1, but the nomenclature is somewhat modified. The ss 013 of 331 Labour economics has been given the extended meaning: "Freedom, dignity, value of labour" and denoted as 331.013.

An extended meaning of ss 01 Philosophy and theory exists in the Main Class 700 Arts

701	Philosophy and theory of fine and decorative arts.
701.1	Appreciative aspects
701.17	Aesthetics.
701.18	Criticism and appreciation of Fine art

In such cases a note indicates "....from Table 1 as modified below"

Classifiers should abstain from giving homemade extended meanings to standard subdivisions, whatsoever the situation be, and howsoever apt the self-extended meaning may appear to be.

Irregular Places

Some standard subdivisions are shown as subject divisions and consequently moved to a division in the array. It happens because that compound subject has a subject value and considerable literary warrant. Such treatment allows the further extension of such subjects. This happens usually for the geographical and historical treatment of a subject:

331 Compensation [for Labour]

331.29 History, geographic treatment, biography of compensation (instead of 331.209).

To avoid cross classification cross references and class else where notes are provided from a probable class number likely to be looked at by the classifier to the actual number used in the Schedules. For example, in the above case, the not used class number [331.2109] is enclosed in square brackets, and a cross reference directs the classifier to 331.29. Similarly, Techniques, apparatus, material for art metal work is 739.1 instead of 739.028, as techniques, apparatus, etc is an ss, but here it has been enumerated like a subject.

Similarly, 720.9 is History, geographical treatment, biography of architecture. But the architectures of specific Ages, instead of being provided in 720.901-.905 have been shifted to 722-724. Accordingly at [720.901—.905] one reads the instructions "Do not use, class in 722-724". Therefore:

Medieval architecture

723 instead of 720.902

Twentieth century architecture

724.6 instead of 720.904

Another interesting aberration occurs at 666.3 Pottery-

Ceramic technology. Here, we are told to add ss at 666.31–.39, instead of at the usual place 666.301–.309. Thus a Journal of pottery will get the class number 666.35, and Teaching and study of pottery will be 666.37, and so on.

There is further exception to this exception.

Further Materials and equipment for Pottery is 666.4 instead of 666.328.

Some other irregularities also occur in the use of the chronological periods in Table 1. In usual cases any chronological period division is to be taken from the Table 1, where the ss 09 has been further subdivided as 0901-0905, broadly enumerating all periods of history. These are obviously attachable to any class number, but for some classes, (for example, 700 Arts, 800 Literature and 900 History) some special period tables have been provided. Therefore, in such cases these special tables are to be used instead of the general one in ss 090. In fact, in case of main classes 800 and 900, the period is a subject facet, instead of being merely a time auxiliary. For example:

20th Century English poetry

821.91 instead of 821.0904

Elizabethan English drama

822.3 instead of 822.09031

History of India in the 1970s

954.05 instead of 954.09047 or even 954.047

England under Elizabeth I

942.055 instead of 942.09031

History of 18th century Germany

943.05 instead of 943.09033

One more interesting irregularity occurs in 340. The usual place for ss here is given as 340.02-.09. For example:

Dictionary of law

340.03

Study and teaching of law

340.07

But the philosophy and theory of law has been placed at 340.1 with its own extended meaning:

340.112	Law and ethics
340.115	Law and society

Extending the irregular use of the standard subdivisions a bit further, we find numerous cases where a geographical facet is made inherent in the structure of the class number. In such cases, the geographical facet is not added through the ss 09. For instance:

General statistics of Europe

314 instead of 310.94

General statistics of France

314.4 instead of 310.944

General statistics of India

315.4 instead of 310.954

At times, a standard subdivision is redundant if the form or viewpoint is inherent in the subject itself:

Dictionary of the English language

423 instead of 420.3 or 423.03

History of India

954 instead of 954.009

Examples of this kind may be multiplied without end.

Enigma of Zeroes

In Table 1 every ss begins with a zero, which is essentially a facet indicator marking the transition from subject division to form division in the class number. The original rules for adding standard subdivisions (though quite simple and uniform in the beginning) have become rather complex in the face of the warping structure of the DDC. Sometimes a featured zero may seem missing, while at others an ss may begin with one, two, or even three zeroes. This has happened to accommodate new subjects. These oddities have been abruptly grafted rather than evolved. Some subjects have been prepositioned to usurp the hereditary place of standard subdivisions. For example, 344.05 is not a Journal of Social law 344. It is the subject division connoting Law of Police services. Similarly, 616.07 is not the study and teaching of diseases, but means pathology.

Since the place for standard subdivisions has been occupied by subject divisions in such cases, the standard subdivisions are so designated as to distinguish them from subject divisions to avoid confusion. This is done by denoting the ss with two zeroes or three zeroes as the need may be. Hence, there is no fixed formula for attaching or identifying an ss. The only formula is to follow the instructions, if any, provided in the Schedules under every class number. In all such abnormal cases, adequate instructions are invariably provided for adding standard subdivisions. Such irregularities have discounted a great deal the mnemonic value of the scheme, and consequently the classifier's efficiency too has been at a stake.

Dictionary of human diseases

616.003.

Philosophy and theory of constitutional law

342.001

Journal of constitutional law

342.005

Encyclopaedia of Indian history

954.003

Special subdivisions of standard subdivisions

Some of the standard subdivision such as 08,0901-0905, and 093-099 have their own table of special subdivisions which can be added to their asterisked subdivisions. For example, under T1-08 Groups of people (p.195, vol.1) all the special subdivisions are applicable to its entire range of subdivisions. These are subdivisions of subdivisions of T1-0181-089. In fact this results in the use of two standard subdivisions simultaneously:

Statistics on the reading habits of children

028.9 (Reading habits) + 083 (T1; children) + 021 (Stat. spl. Subdiv. under T1- 08) =028.9083021

Reading habits of teenager girls in India

028.9 + 08352 (T1; teenager girls) + 09 (spl. Subdiv. under-08 (T1)) + 54 (T2; as instructed under 09) = 028.908352 0954

Museums of ancient Buddhism in Japan

294.3+ 0901 (T1) + 074 (spl. subdivision) + 52 (T2) =294.3090107452

Similarly, under T1-093-099 there is a table of special subdivisions (p. 209, vol.1) which can be added to all its subdivisions.

Statistics on private publishing in India

070.593 + 09 (T1) + 54 (T2) + 021 (spl. subdivision) = 070.5930954021

Museum of Indian Dolls in the UK

745.59221 + 09 (T1) + 54 (T2) + 074 (Museums; spl. subdivision) +41(T2;UK) = 745.59221095407441

Rules for adding Standard Subdivisions

Subject to the above rules, a standard subdivision may be added to any class number. If the ultimate class number is a Main class having, two zeroes or a Division having one zero, then these filler-zeroes are removed while adding the standard subdivision. For example, take the title "Encyclopaedia of Science". Science is 500, and Encyclopaedia is a ss with notation 03. Since in 500 there are two filler zeroes, these are to be removed. The synthesised class number is:

500+03= 5+03 = 503

Similarly,

Journal of philosophy

100+05=1+05 = 105

In 510, Mathematics, we have only one filler zero, so, it is to be removed while adding any standard subdivision:

History of mathematics

510+09=51+09=510.9

Philosophy of mathematics

510+01=51+01=510.1

The reader may be reminded here that zero/zeroes removed are those belonging to class number, not to the standard subdivision. The featured zero of the ss is always there.

These filler zeroes are not to be removed, or removed only partially, as the occasion may demand, if the subject divisions have been moved to the places of ss. For example

Dictionary of social sciences

300.3 and not 303

Here only one zero of 300 has been removed, though there are two redundant or filler zeroes in 300 social sciences. This has been done because the class number 303 has already been assigned the meaning of Social process in Sociology.

Similarly, 532.005 is a Journal of fluid mechanics instead of 532.05, which means fluid dynamics here. Here (under 532) instructions have been provided to use ss as 532.001-532.009. Such instructions do not have hierarchic force, i.e. ss to the subdivisions of 532 are to be added with normal zeroes, as there will be no ambiguity.

Journal of Fluid dynamics

532.0505 instead of 532.05005

Research in Fluid statics

532.02072 instead of 532.020072

Here are given some examples to illustrate the variety and scope and standard subdivisions.

Apparatus and equipment for circulation services in a library

025.60284

Library and information science profession

020.23

A dictionary of Acronyms in library and information science

020.148, not 020.3

(By applying Table of precedence given in T1 (p. 180, vol. 1)

Indian history through pictures

954.00222

History of Mughal India through pictures

954.0250222

A Video on the DDC

025.4310208

A Video on the history of the DDC

025.4310208, not 025.43109

History of the DDC up to the end of the 19th century

025.43109034

Exercises in the DDC

025.431076

Many of the standard subdivisions may be further extended by synthesis either through Tables 2, 5, 6, 7, or from the Schedules:

Boolean principles of Internet searching.

025.0425+015(T1)+11324 (from the class number 511.324 Boolean) = 025.042501511324

Here 015 Scientific principles is a standard subdivision which is to be further divided like 510-590; and Boolean algebra is 511.324

Indian Library Association

020.622+54 (Table 2) =020.62254

The class number for a national library organisation is 020.622 to which area notation from Table 2 is to be added as per instructions.

Universities imparting library science education in Maharashtra State.

020.711+5479 (T2)=020.7115479

Under Tl-07 education -0711 is an ss for college and universities which is further extendable by area.

Research in library classification in Canada

025.42+072+0+71=025.42072071

Life of Melvil Dewey by Fremont A. Rider

020.92

Autobiography of S R Ranganathan

020.92

Dictionary of philosophy

100+03=103

History of philosophy in India

100+09+54=109.54

(It is not the history of Indian philosophy). Here the ss 09 has been extended by the Area Table.

Reader advisory services to Medicos

025.54+088(T1)+61(From 610 Medical science)= 025.5408861

Here, the subject has been treated with respect to doctors (a non-ethnic, regardless of national groups of people). Here ss 088 has been extended by 001-999 where medical science is 610.

Reading interests of Physicians

028.9+088+61 (from 610 schedules)=028.908861

but

Reading interests of children

028.53+4(From T1-0832-0835) =028.534

Here the use of ss 08 for children will be redundant, as the class number itself means young people by age group.

Reading habits of Indians (national group)

028.9+089+91411(Table5)=028.908991411

089 is the ss for treatment of the subject among national groups, which is to be further extended by the Table 5, where the number for Indians is 91411. The use of ss 088 and 089 should be distinguished from -024 which means a work for specific type of users by profession.

Natural science for social scientists

500 + 024 (T1) + 300 = 502.43

Mathematical statistics for librarians

519.502402 i.e., 519.5 + 024 (T1) +02 (from 020 schedules)

Arithmetic for business managers

513.024658

Participation of Indian soldiers in World War II battles in France

World War II battles in Europe

940.5421

This is further divisible by T2-41-49

World War II battles in France

940.5421+4(from T2-44) = 940.54214

To the result we will use T5 for Indian

via the ss-089. Hence

940.54214+089(T1) +91411(T5)

= 940.5421408991411

Political conditions of the world in the 21st century: A short term forecast

320+0905 (T1) + 01 (special Table under ss-09-on p. 203 vol. 1) =320.90501 (one filler zero has been removed)

Political conditions of India: A forecast

320.95401

Marxian economics in the 1950s

335.409045

Marxian economics in the USSR in the 1950s

335.4+09(T1) + 47(T2) + 045 (from 09045 Table 1) =335.40947045

6

Use of Table 2: Geographic Areas, Historical Periods, Biography

Whenever a subject is studied within the context of a given geographic area, the ultimate class number is qualified by the area number taken from Table 2. In some subjects such as general statistics, history, geography, etc the area is already embedded in the class number. For example, 315 General statistics of Asia. Here the digit 5 is for Asia. The need to add area notation usually occurs in the social sciences and the humanities where the treatment and practice of a subject varies from place to place. Some other disciplines may also need the area facet occasionally. Where the schedule does not authorise us to add from the area table, the area table can still be added through ss 09 from Table 1.

This is largest of all the auxiliary tables (pp. 210 to 636 out of the total of 582 pages devoted to all the six tables); the largeness consists not in any variety of subdivisions as it is in details. A brief paragraph of instructions (p. 210) precedes enumeration of area numbers. All areas of the world, natural geographical divisions, or political or administrative units, or some scattered geophysical divisions of the earth or some noncontiguous conceptual divisions based on various characteristics of people who habitat them, have been accommodated in divisions 1 to 9. The area 1 stands for the scattered regions bound by some geophysical characteristic or by some socio-cultural characteristics, e.g., plane regions, forests, deserts, oceans, socio-economic regions, and so on. The digit 2 has been allotted to biographies regardless of areas, region, places. Notation 3 denotes the ancient world; and the modem world as divided into various continents has been denoted by digits 4 to 9. Obviously the details for the geographical subdivisions of area numbers for the USA 73-79 are far more deep than those of any other country. Here subdivisions have been enumerated down to county, and even city level, whereas for many countries, there are no further divisions at all.

The area number is added to the ultimate class number, though some classes are directly based on the geographical characteristic, so the area number is inherent there; for example, in history 954 is the history of India, 973 is history of the USA, as-54 and -73 are area numbers as taken from the area table; similarly 314 is general statistics of Europe and 315 is general statistics of Asia, where 4 and 5 respectively are the area numbers of Europe and Asia.

Use of Table 2 for area does not pose any difficulty. Whenever a class number needs extension by geographical area, there are sufficient instructions in the schedules to do so. Occasionally, a division (usually at 9 in the array) is left for geographical and historical treatment of the subject:

Political conditions

320.9

(As per instructions, this class number is to be further subdivided by the area number 1 to 9 from Table 2)

Political conditions of India

320.954 i.e., 320.9 + 54 (T2),

Political conditions in Rajasthan

320.9+544(T2) 320.9544

Political conditions in the.USA

320.973

Political conditions in Christian countries

320.91761 i.e., 320.9 + 1761 (T2)

Sometimes a class number itself is to be directly divided by the area number:

Constitutional law of Canada

342+71 (T2) = 342.71

Japanese Diet (Parliament)

328+52 (T2) = 328.52

Foreign policy of Britain

327+41(T2) = 327.41

Here class numbers 342, 328, and 327 have been divided by the area numbers 71, 52, and 41 respectively.

Adding Area without Instruction

Where there is no instruction but the subject of the document under classification requires the addition of an area number from Table 2, then the area number is added to the class number via ss 09. Latter works as a facet indicator:

Child labour in India – an economic study

331.31 + 09 (T1) + 54 (T2) = 331.310954

Men's costumes in the Himachal Pradesh

391.1095452 i.e., 391.1 + 09 (T1) + 5452 (T2)

Freedom of speech in former Communist countries

323.443+09+1717(T2) = 323.443091717

Standard of living in rural areas

339.47+09+1734(T2) = 339.47091734

INFLIBNET (India)

004.678 + 09 + 54 (T2) = 004.6780954

So, an area number may be added to any class number by either of the two ways depending upon whether there is an invitation or not to add from the area table.

Adding Area through 0 only

Sometimes, an area number may be added through 0 instead of 09. For example, at 920.03-.09 biographies by specific geographical areas.

Biographies of persons living in India

920+0+54(T2) = 920.054

Here, as per instructions, the area number 54 for India has been added to the base number 920.0

Biographies of persons living in Rajasthan

920.0544

Libraries in the USA

027.073

(General) Libraries in Pennsylvania

027.0748

If a subject is a study extending to two non-adjacent areas, we cannot add area numbers for both; we will have to choose one.

Democracy in India and the USA

321.80954 or 321.80973

If, however, there is an interaction between two different areas, then the Schedules sometimes provide a mechanism to join them:

Foreign relations between India and the USA

327.54+0+73=327.54073

Here, as per instructions, the class number 327 is to be subdivided by the first area, then 0 is to be added and to the result the area number for the second geographical area is to be added.

Similarly,

India's foreign policy towards non-aligned countries

327.54+0+1716=327.5401716

Trade agreements between India and the USA

382.954073 = 382.9 + 54 (T2) + 0 +73 (T2)

Migration from India to the USA

304.8+73(T2)+0+54(T2)=304.873054

Migration from Asia to Europe

304.8+4+0+5 = 304.8405

Country of destination is the first facet and the country of origin is the last facet.

Cases where Area is already a part of the class number

Sometimes, a geographical facet is inherent in the subject, therefore, it appears, as a subject division in the class number:

History of India

954

General statistics of Asia

315

In such cases, these class numbers can further be divided by the area table to provide class numbers in respect of subordinate areas.

History of Rajasthan

954.4 .

General statistics of India*

315.4 4

General statistics of Rajasthan*

315.44

(544 is the number for Rajasthan in Table 2)

A class number extended by an area notation can also admit a chronological subdivision. In such cases, we are only required to add the subdivision of 09 in 0901-0905 from Table 1 or by the special chronological subdivisions, if provided:

History of Mughal India

954.025

History of Rajasthan under the Mughals

9+544(T2) +025 (from 954.025) = 954.4025

Historical and geographical treatment of science

509

History of science in India

500+09(T1)+54(T2) =509.54

Two zeroes in 500 have been dropped in the final synthesis

History of science in India in 20th century

509.54 + 0904(T1) = 509.540904

General statistics of Asia in the 19th Century

315+09034(T1) = 315.09034

Political conditions in India in the 1980s

320.954+09048 = 320.95409048

More such examples are given in Chapter 13 of this book

Sometimes, an area may be further extended by the special subject divisions as in the cases of 340 Law and 350 Public Administration:

Military, tax, trade, industrial law

343

Income tax law

343.052

Indian income tax law

343 + 54 (T2) + 052 (from 343.052) =343.54052

(see instruction under 093-099 of 342-347, p. 558, vol.2)

Here 343 has first been divided by country (India-54) then the resulting class number has been further extended by the subject division 052 Income tax of 343.

Similarly:

Law of public health

344.04

Indian law of public health

344.5404

US law of public health

344.7304

US Law of Public Health in New York State

344.7304+09+747=344.730409747

Prime minister (in the cabinet form of government)

352.23

The prime minister of India

352.230954

Queen of Britain

352.2330941

Separate provision of the area table since the 17th edition (1967) has facilitated the division of the earth and population clusters from various conceptual viewpoints. These are various physiogeographic and socio-economic regions, all shown as subdivisions of 1:

Standard of living in villages

339.47+09+1734(T2) =339.47091734

Atmospheric pressure in mountains

551.54+09+143=551.5409143

Here 143 is mountains from the Area table added through the ss 09.

As per instructions given under -1 (Table 2, p.212, vol. 1) each subdivision of the 1 area has the option to be qualified by any country 3-9 from the same area table by using 0 as a facet indicator. This enhances the versatility of the scheme:

Standard of living in Indian villages

339.47+09+1734(T2)+0+54(T2)=339.47091734054

Atmospheric pressure in Indian mountains

551.54+09+143(T2)+0+54(T2)=551.5409143034*

Political conditions in Communist countries

320.91717

Political conditions in communist countries of Asia*

320.9+1717(T2)+0+5(T2)=320.9171705

Political conditions in Christian countries of Africa*

320.9+1761(T2)+0+6(T2)=320.9176106

Here all the subdivisions of 1 have been further extended by the area number from 3-9 via 0 which acts as a facet indicator. Bear in mind, however, these five examples are optional, not standard.

Use of T2 with other Tables

Some of the divisions may further be subdivided by some of the other auxiliary tables. For example -174 Regions where specific ethnic, national groups predominate: obviously this number is further divisible by the auxiliary Table 5:

Places where Punjabi people predominate

- 174(T2)+9142(T5)= -1749142

Social status of women in the regions where Punjabi people predominate

305.42+09+1749142=305.42091749142

Similarly, division -175 Regions where specific languages predominate:

Reading habits in English-speaking people

028.9+09+175 (Table 2)+21 (Table 6) = 028.90917521

Here area division 175 (added via 09) has been further divided by Table 6, where the number for the English language is 21.

Hospitality of Punjabi people

395.3+09(T2)+175(T2)+9142(T6)=395.3091759142

Here area 175 added via 09 has been extended by Table 6, where 9142 is the number for the Punjabi language.

Similarly, area 176 can be further extended by religion as taken from 292-299 in the schedules:

School discipline in Muslim countries

371.5+09+176(Table 2)+7 (From 297 schedules, vol. 2)=371.5091767

Here to 176 we have added the digits following 29 in 292-299 where the number for Islam is 297.

Restricted range of Area Numbers to be added

In the schedules many a time instructions specify to "add areas notation 3-9 from Table 2". It only means that the areas denoted by the subdivisions 1 and 2 fall outside the jurisdiction of such instructions. In such cases, we cannot add directly areas from subdivisions 1 and 2 (Table 2). If needed we can add such class numbers via the ss 09. For example, Foreign policy of non-aligned nations cannot leave the fol1owing number:

327.1716

The correct number is 327.091716

Similarly,

Parliaments in non-aligned nations

328.091716

Civil rights in Communist countries

323.091717

7

Use of Table 3: Subdivisions for the Arts, for Individual Literatures, For Specific Literary Forms

As the name of this auxiliary table implies, this table is mostly meant for the main class 800 Literature.* Since the 20th edition (1989) Table 3 has been divided into three sub tables, viz, 3A, 3B, and 3C.

Table 3A is for works by or about individual authors.

Table 3B is for works by or about more than two authors.

Table 3C is to be used in conjunction with Table 3B and in 808-809.

It may be pointed out that the subdivisions enumerated in these three Tables are not new or unfamiliar. These three tables make easy the mode of addition of facets without increasing their scope.

Table 3A is the simplest of the three tables since

individual authors are permitted only the facets of literary form and period. Table 3B is far more complicated.

Table 3B consists of the Standard Subdivisions in conformity with Table 1 and from divisions 1-8. Here the ss-08 can be further extended by Table 3C. The ss 09 History, description, critical appraisal is applicable to the body of literature regardless of form or language in which the literature is written. **The ss 09 is extendable either by the period tables, or by some literary viewpoints taken from Table 3C but not by both, if no form of literature is given.** It may be noted that time period is to be taken not from Table 1, as each language literature has its own special period tables. Therefore, both standard subdivisions 08 and 09 are somewhat modified forms of the standard subdivisions here. The hard core of the table consists of the various forms of literature, which are the same for every literature irrespective of the language in which it is written:

- -1 Poetry
- -2 Drama
- -3 Fiction
- -4 Essays
- -5 Speeches
- -6 Letters
- -7 Satire and humour
- -8 Miscellaneous writings

Each form subdivision has further been subdivided into its various kinds and further into varieties, if any. These scopes/kinds/varieties of literary forms have been further subdivided through a single zero, and the ss are also applicable to the form divisions through double zeroes. For example, take the form division 3 Fiction:

- 3001-3009 Standard subdivisions; collection; history, description, critical

	appraisal
- 301-308	Fiction of specific scope and kinds
- 301	Short stories
- 308	Specific kinds of fiction
- 3081	Historical and period fiction
- 3083	Psychological, realistic sociological fiction
-3085	Love and romance
-3087	Adventure fiction

31-39 is fiction of specific periods. Bare (unextended) form divisions 1-8 are divisible by the period divisions specific to each language literature. Kinds of forms do not admit period facet. Take, for example the case of English fiction:

- 31 Fiction of Early English Period
- 32 Fiction of Pre-Elizabethan Period
- 33 Fiction of Elizabethan Period
- 34 Fiction of Post-Elizabethan(Restoration) Period
- 35 Fiction of Queen Anne Period
- 36 Fiction of Later 18th Century
- 37 Fiction of early 19th Century Romantic period
- 38 Fiction of Victorian Period
- 39 Fiction of 20th Century
- 392 Fiction of 21st Century

Similarly, for, say, Hindi fiction the periods are as follow:

- 31 Hindi Fiction up to 1345
- 32 Hindi Fiction from 1345-1645
- 33 Hindi Fiction from 1645-1845
- 34 Hindi Fiction from 1845-1895
- 35 Hindi Fiction from 1895-1919
- 36 Hindi Fiction from 1920-1939

- 37 Hindi Fiction after 1940-

- 371 Hindi Fiction 1940-1999

- 372 Hindi Fiction of 21st Century

After the period division, we can further add the special ss as given in Table 3B.

Main class 800 has many facets, viz., language, form, period, standard subdivision, the latter being further extendable by a variety of viewpoints or topics. In view of the multiplicity of facets, their citation order presents some complications especially when not all the facets are present. Language, form, and period are the core facets in their decreasing order of importance. Let us discuss the various cases one by one.

I. When the language facet is absent

The study of literature in general falls in the sections 801 to 809. It is clear that these are the standard subdivisions (of course modified) as applied to the bare main class:

801 Philosophy and theory [of Literature]

802 Miscellany

803 Dictionaries, encyclopaedias, etc.,

805 Serial publications

806 Organisations and management

807 Education, research, related topics

808 Rhetoric and collections of literary texts from more than two literatures

809 History, description, critical appraisal of more than two literatures.

Subdivisions of 801 and part of 808 have been enumerated in the schedules; some synthesis is also possible here. However, the citation order in 808.8 "Collections of literary texts from more than two literatures" needs some illustrations. The citation formula is

Base number 808.8+Form+Period (from Table 1)

Collections from 20th century literature (regardless of form and language)

808.8001-.8005 Collections from specific periods.

As per instructions here, we are to add to the base number 808.800, the number following 090 in 0901-0905 from Table 1 (of Standard Subdivisions). The number for the 20th century is 0904, and the digit following 090 is "4" only. Hence the class number is

808.800+4=808.8004

Similarly:

Collection of 17th century World literature

808.800+31=808.80031

Selections from literature of the 1970s

808.800+47=808.80047

Collections of poetry

808.81

Collections of World poetry from the 1970s

808.81+0+47=808.81047

808.81 is collections of poetry. This number is an asterisked number. As per instructions given under 808.8101-808.8105 (p. 779, vol.3) we have added to 808.81 the notation for period as explained there. Again the period has been taken from the general period table, viz, Table 1 Standard subdivisions. **As a rule, when no language is given, the time period is to be taken from Table 1.**

It may be noted that period division now can be added to the collections of some specific forms of literature or displaying some specific feature.

Collection of 20th century epic poetry

808.812-.817 Collection of Specific kind of poetry

As given under 102-107(T3, pp. 652-653, vol.1) + 00904 (T3C))

808.81 + 32 (from 1032 T3B) + 09 as given under 102 - 107 (p.628, vol. 1) + 00904 (T3C)

= 808.81320900904

Collection of 20th century one act plays

808.822-.825 Collection of Specific kind of drama

808.82+41 (from 2041 T3B) + 09 (As mentioned under -102-107 (T3B)) + 00904 (T3C) (-00901-00905 T3C, p. 665, vol. 1)

= 808.82410900904

II. When the language facet is present

Literatures of specific languages are placed in 810-890, and the language makes the first facet in the citation order. An introduction to the procedure for building a class number for any language literature has been explained in the schedules on pages v3:793 and fully at the beginning of Tables 3A and 3B and in the Manual, vol. 1, pp. 154-159,638-639 and 644-646.

A combination of main class digit 8 and the language constitutes the compound facet, which is termed as the base number. It is the base to which all other facets are added in an ordained order. Base numbers for almost all the languages have been enumerated and specifically indicated at 810-890. For certain languages, this base number can be built with the help of language numbers taken from Table 6 Languages:

For example:

891.99	Other Indo-European literatures
891.991	Albanian
891.892	Armenian
891. 993-.998	Others

Here the instruction reads: Add to 891.99 the numbers

following -9199 in notation 91993-91998 from Table 6, e.g., Hittite 891.998 (from 91998 Hittite Table 6). In this way, the class number for Tocharian language literature is 891.994. Similarly 891.991 is Albanian literature (from 91991 Table 6).

These numbers can further be extended by Table 3A.

To the available base number in the schedules, we add the facets in the following order :

Base number +Form [Table 3A] +Period + ss 08 or 09 (Subject/ viewpoint from Table 3B) +T3C

It is obvious that in a given literary work all the above facets may not be present all the time. Whenever Tables 3A or 3B are to be used, such base numbers are marked with an asterisk or given instruction to add from Table 3. For major literatures readymade c1ass numbers adding the form facet have been-enumerated.

For example:

821	English poetry
822	English drama
827	English satire and humor
861	Spanish poetry
862	Spanish drama
863	Spanish fiction
864	Spanish essays
865	Spanish speeches
866	Spanish letters
867	Spanish satire and humor.
868	Spanish miscellaneous writings

Instructions to use Tables 3A and 3B to construct a complete class number have been explained in a programmatic manner preceding the Tables. These instructions have made the facet structure quite transparent, though the instructions do not make very easy reading mostly due to the multiplicity of facets and various means of applying them:

In the case of individual authors the standard subdivisions and their further extension by Tables 3B and 3C is not admissible. For individual authors the formula is: Base + T3A + Period (from Schedules)

Hence books by and on an individual author get the same number.

For example:

A critical study of John Keats's poetry

(He was an English poet of the early 19th century) 82 (Base) + 1 (Form Poetry) +7 (Period from v3:799)

= 82+1+7=821.7

(Here we cannot add the ss for criticism)

Similarly, a study of plot construction in the novels of Thomas Hardy will get the class number as follows:

82 (Base) +3 (Form, Fiction from Table 3A) + 8 (Period from v3: 799)

=82+3+8=823.8

Here, the critical element Plot construction will have to be ignored. Any work of fiction by Hardy or any work on Hardy as a fiction writer will get the class number 823.8. Not only this the various Victorian novelists, such as Hardy, George Eliot, Thackeray, Dickens, and Mrs. Gaskell can only be differentiated through book numbers as they all will get the same class number 823.8.

III. In case the form facet is absent

In works by or about more than two authors (Table 3B) the citation formula takes the following order:

For collections of works with a specific theme :

Base Number+080(T3B) +Table 3 C

For critical studies:

Base Number+0900+Period for that specific literature; or Base number +09+Table 3C for theme or viewpoint.

A Collection of Hindi literature with love theme [More than form and no period]

891.430+80(T3B)+3543(T3C)=891.430803543

Collection of Hindi literature on tragedy

891.430+80+162 (T3C)=891.43080162

Critical study of characters in English literature [No Form, No Period]

820+9(T3B)+27(T3C)=820.927

History of 20th century English literature

820+900(T3B)+91 (from p. 799, vol.3)=820.90091

In the facet formula, the third facet is the time period in which the author flourished as a writer. It may be noted that in case of a specific language literature, the period is not to be taken from ss 09 of Table 1. For every language literature special period divisions enumerating epochs of that particular literature have been given in the Schedules (Vol. 3) at the beginning of each language literature. For example, for Modern Indian literatures the period table given under 891.4 is:

1	Early period to 1345.
2	1345-1645
3	1645-1845
4	1845-1895
5	1895-1919
6	1920-1939
7	1940-
71	1940-1999
72	2000-

One thing more to be noted about the period table is that in case the literature in that language is written in more than one country, then different period tables are given for each major country. For example, for French literature different period tables exist for Asian and African countries, for Belgium, for Canada and, of course, for France. Their necessity is obvious, as each country has different epochs in its literary history. For instance, for French language literature the period table for French is:

For Asian and African countries

1	Early period to 1959
2	1960-1999
3	2000-

For Belgium

1	Early Period to 1829
2	1830-1899
3	1900-1999
32	1900-1945
34	1945-1999
4	2000-

For Canada

3	Colonial period to 1867
4	1867-1899
5	1900-1999
52	1900-1945
54	1945-1999
6	2000-

For France

1	Early period to 1399

2	1400-1499
3	Renaissance period, 1500-1599
4	Classical period, 1600-1715
5	18th century, 1715-1789
6	1789-1815
7	Constitutional monarchy, 1815-1848
8	1848-1899
9	1900-
91	1990-1999
912	1900-1945
914	1945-1999
92	2000-

After adding the period division, the ss may be added. Detailed instructions have been provided to give step by step guidance. A period division is further extendable by standard subdivisions as taken from 1001-1009 (T3B). Here the ss begins only with a single zero, as per rule. If needed, these ss, especially 08 and 09, may further be extended by viewpoint Table 3C. For example:

Collection of Victorian Poetry. (English Poetry of the late nineteenth century):

Base (English language literature)	82
Poetry (Form, Table 3B)	1 (from-11-19)
Victorian period (v.3: 777)	8
Collection (as Instructed under 11-19)	08(from-1001-1009) Table 3B)

Hence the complete class number is

821.808

Similarly:

Critical appraisal of Victorian fiction

82 Base Number

+3 (T3B, Fiction of specific period)

+8 (Victorian Period, from Vol. 3: 799)

+09 (As under 1001-1009 T3B, p. 650, Vol. 1)

=823.809

Social themes in Victorian Fiction

For critical appraisal of Victorian fiction, we have 823.809. Since 08 and 09 are further extendable by Table 3C, we can add to the result the appropriate notation for social themes from Table 3C which is 355. Hence the complete class number is

823.809+355=823.809355

Critical study of plots in post-war American novels: 81(Base) +3 (Form) +54 (Period) +

+09(Critical appreciation 10091-1099, Table 3B,p.650, vol.3) +24 (Plot, Table 3C)

=81+3+54+09+24=813.540924

More examples will help to clarify further :

American literature

810

Dictionary of American literature

81+03(ss-03 from 01-07 T3B)=810.3*

(Note that the base for American literature is 81) International Conference on American literature

81+0601(ss-0601 from T3B) =810.601*

All India Conference on American Literature*

81+060(Tl-0603-0609)+54(T2)=810.6054

(We have added-54 from Table 2 to the base number 060 from Table 1. This has been done as per instructions under ss-0603-0609 in Table 1)

History of American literature of the Colonial period

810+900(from 09001-09009,T3B) +1=810.9001

Here 1 (Colonial period) has been added from the period table for American literature given at v3:795

History of 20th century American literature

810+900+5=810.9005

History of American literature for children

810+9(from 091-099,T3B)+9282 notation for children in Table 3C =810+9+9282=810.99282

History of realism in American literature

810+9+12 (Table 3C realism) =810+9+12=810.912

American poetry

810+1(from T3B)=811

Dictionary of American poetry

81+1003(-1001-1007,T3B)=811.003

All India Conference on American Poetry

81+1006(T3B)+0+54(T2)=81+1006054=811.006054

History of American poetry

81+1009 (T3B)=811.009

History of American poetry in 19th century

81+1009034(from100901-100907, T3B)

+811.009034

American epic poetry

81+1032(T3B, p. 652, vol.1)=811.032

Dictionary of American epic poetry

81+1032+03 Dictionary (as per instructions under T3B-102 -107, p. 651 vol.1)=811.03203

All India Conference on American Epic Poetry

81+1032+06054=811.03206054

History of American epic poetry

81+1032+09=811.03209

History of American epic poetry in 19th century

81+1032+090(T3B from 0901-0909)

+3 from(811-818,p. 795, vol.3)

=811.0320903

Realism in American epic poetry of 20th century: A critical appraisal

Base, American Literature	=81
Epic poetry (Table 3B)	=1032
Critical appraisal (from T3B-102-107)	=09
Period Table 3C (from 01-09)	=0
20th century (from special Table at 795 p. vol. 3)	=5
811.0320905	

It may be noted here the "Realism" Facet had to be ignored to accommodate period facet for 20th century.

If we include realism then the period facet i.e. 20th century will have to be ignored :

Base	81
Epic poetry	1032(T3B)
Critical study	09(from 091-099under -102-107 in T3B,vol. 1,p.648)
Realism	-12 (from T3C)
	=811.0320912*

Classification of literary works without language or form

Collections from 20th century literature

808.8	Collection from more than two literatures
808.8001-.8005	Collection from specific periods

As per instructions, we are to add to the base number 808.800 the number following 090 in ss notation 0901-0905 from Table 1 = 808.800+4 =808.8004.

(The reader is again reminded here that the period has been taken from the general period table, viz, Table 1.)

Collection of literature on social themes

Collection displaying specific features.

808.801-.803

Here, we are to add to the base number 808.80 notation 1-3 from Table 3C. In Table 3C the notation for social themes is 355. Hence the required class number is

808.80+355(T3C) =808.80355

Collection of epic poetry

(No language and period)

808.81 Collection of poetry

808.812-.817 Collection of specific kinds of poetry

As per instructions here (p. 779, vol. 3) we are to add to the base number 808.81 the numbers following 10 in 102- 107 of Table 3B. The notation for epic poetry is 1032. So, as per instructions we are to add 32 to the base 808.81

808.81+32=808.8132

Use of Table 3 C

Critical appraisal of Romanticism in 19th century English poetry

82+1+8+09+145=821.809145

Base: English literature =82

Poetry (of specific period) =1

-11-19, T3B

19th century as under 82 1-828 =8

(Schedules vol. 3, p. 799)

Critical appraisal (from10091-10099) = 09 (from 1009 T3B)

Romanticism (T3C) = 145

821.809145

Portrayals of children in Victorian English fiction (Period is later 19th century: the Victorian period): [Critical Study is implied]

82+3(T3B from 31-39) +8(Period) +09 (from 10091-10099 in T3B) +352(T3C) +3 (from 083, Table 1)

=823.8093523

Religious themes in English drama of the Queen Anne Period

82+2+5+0+9+382

=822.509382

Depiction of ancient Indian civilization in Victorian fiction

823+ 8 + 09 (10091-10099,T3B)+ 3582(T3C) +934 (from 934 schedule)

=823.8093582934

Collection of English literature written by Asians [No Form, No Period]

82+080 (from 0801-0809,T3B) +8 (From 81-89,Table 3C) +914 (Table 5)

=820.808914

21st Century French literature – a critical appraisal

840+900(from 09001-09009,T3B)+92 (For later 21st Century as under 841-848, vol. 3)

=840.90092

Romanticism in English poetry

82+1009(from -10091-10099, T3B) + 145(T3C) = 821.009145

Plot in 17th century Spanish novels

86+3+3(Period)+09(from-10091-10099,T3B) +24 (Table 3C)

=863.30924

Description of intelligensia in 20th Century English novels

82+3+91(20th century)+09(from-10091-10099, T3B) + 352 (Table3C) + 6222(from 086222, Table 1) = 823.91093526222

Collection of German language literature written by Englishmen

[No Form, No Period]

83+080(from 0801-0809 T3B)+8(Table 3C)+21

(Table 5)=830.80821

Collection of German language literature by Jews

83+080+(T3B)+8+924 (Table 5)=830.808924

Depiction of Indian religions in English literature [No Form, No Period]

820+9(T3B, 091-099) +4(Table 3C)+294 (from the Schedules 001-999) = 820.94294

A critical study of plots in Hindi novels of the early 20th century

891.43	Hindi Literature
3	Fiction (T3B)
71	Period under 891.4 (vol. 3, p. 832)
09	from 10091-10099 T3B, vol. 1, p. 627
24	For plot in T3C
	= 891.433710924

Contributions to Hindi literature by Bengalis – a critical study (no form, no period))

891.430(from 891.4301-891.4309)+9(from 091-099 in Table 3B)

+8 (literature for and by various specific ethnic,

national groups from Table 3C)

As per instructions, 8 is to be further subdivided by Table 5, where the notation for Bengali people is 9144

Hence the complete number is

891.43098+9144 (Table 5)=891.430989144

Contributions of Bengalis to Hindi poetry (no period)

891.43 + 1009(from 10091-10099 T3B) + 8(T3C) + 9144(T5)

=891.43100989144

The contribution of Bengalis to Hindi poetry of the post 1940 era

891.43+1+71 (Period) +09 (from10091-10099 T3B) +Table 3C+ Table 5

=891.43+1+71 (Period) +09 +8 (by various national, ethnic groups, Table 3C) +9144 (for Bengalis from Table 5)

=891.431710989144

Depiction of Hinduism in British English fiction

82+300 (from-3001-3009 T3B) +9 (from 10091-10099 T3B) + 382 (T3C) + 945 (from 294.5 Hinduism) = 823.009382945

Hinduism in 20th century British fiction

Base: English literature	=	82
Fiction (of specific period) (T3B)	=	3
20th Century as under 820	=	91
Critical study	=	09(from 10091 -10099 T3B) T3B, p. 650 vol. 1)
Religious themes (Table 3C)	=	382
Hinduism from 294.5	=	945

823.9109382945

Collection of Hindi literature for children [No Form, No Period]

891.430(from891.4301-891.4309)+80 (from -0801-0809 of Table 3B)+9282 (Table 3C)

=891.430809282

Collection of Hindi poetry for children

891.43+10080(from-100801-100809 of T3B p.650,vol. 1) + 9282 (T3C)

= 891.43100809282

Collection of 21st Century Hindi poetry for children

891.43+1+72 (Period) +080(from 1001-1009 T3B) +9282(Table 3C)

=891.431720809282

A critical study of women novelists of the Victorian period

82+3(T3B) +8 (Victorian Period) + 09 (from 10091-10099) + 9287 (Women, T3C)

= 823.8099287

The reader may be again reminded that the elements from Table 3 can only be added when instructed to do so in the Schedules. Where a number admits notation from Table 3, such a number is marked with an asterisk or given explicit instructions. The number cannot be extended further where there are no such instructions.

For example,

Chattisgarhi (Hindi) literature

891.492

If we have Chattisgarhi poetry, the class number is still

891.492

Anthology of Kashmiri literature

891.499

Anthology of Bagheli poetry

841.49

(Here no other facet is admissible)

Let us take some more examples:

Stream of Consciousness in 20th century English novels

82+3+91+ 09 +25=823.910925

Anthology of French poems composed in India (Here there is no period division)

Base number for French literature 84

Collection of poetry 10080(from 100801-100809, T3B)

For Indians, as per instruction, the number is to be taken from 93-99 of Table 3C. Here 9 is the base to be further extended by Table 2, thus, the number for Indians is

- 9+54=-954

Making 10080 as the base, we add to it the number for Indians:

84+10080+954=841.0080954

Collection of Hindi lyrical love poetry [No Period]

891.43+104+08(from 081-089,T3B)+3543

=891.43104083543

Critical appraisal of Punjabi satirical poetry by writers living in Canada

891.42	Punjabi literature
107	Satirical poetry (T3B)
09	(as under - 102 - 107 under T3B, vol. 1, p. 652)
9	(from 93-99 in T3C, p. 677, vol. 1)
71	(Canada, T2)
	= 891.4210709971

Collection of English literature written by children

Base = 820

Collection = 80 (from 0801-0809 Table 3B)

Here we have the instructions to go to Table 3C where number of children writers is 9282: 82+080+9282=820.809282

Critical Appraisal of Hindi short stories written by Punjabis

Base number for Hindi literature 891.43

Short Stories 301(T3B)

To this we have to add as under-102-107 (T3B,vol 1, p.651)

Critical appraisal (from 091-099 T3B) 09

Literature for and by various specific racial ethnic national groups 8

8 is further extended by notations 03-99 from Table 5, where the number for Punjabis is 91421

Hence the complete number is

891.43+301+09+8+91421=891.4330109891421

A critical appraisal of the poetry of Rabindranath Tagore

891.44+1+5 (Period) =891.4415

Use of Table 3C outside the main class 800

Comedy motion pictures

791.4361+7 (from 17 T3C) = 791.43617

Comedy TV programmes

791.456-1+7(from 17, T3C) =791.45617

8

Use of Table 4: Subdivisions of Individual Languages and Language Families For the Languages Schedule, (400)

This, one of the simplest tables to use, is exclusively used for the Main Class 400 Languages. If need be, it may be extended by the Table 6 Languages. Table 4 lists linguistic aspects, description, analysis and elements.

Main Class digit 4 and the language number taken together form the base. The base numbers for all the major languages have been enumerated in the schedules. The base number is further extendable by Table 4 and, if further need be, by Table 6. The facet formula that emerges is:

Base number + Table 4+Table 6

Whenever Table 4 or Table 6 is to be used, sufficient instructions guide us at 420-490 by marking the base number with an asterisk or giving direct and clear instructions:

Grammar of English Language

Base number for English = 42

Grammar (Table 4) = 5 = 425

(As instructed under 420-490, p. 939, vol. 2)

A study of spellings of the Sanskrit language

Base number for Sanskrit 491.2

Spellings (Table 4) 813= 491.2813

Hindi primer (reader) for semi literates

491.43+862(T4) = 491.43862

Hindi primer for Engineers

491.43+864024(T4)+62(001-999)

= 491.4386402462

It may be noted that here instead of an * asterisk direct instructions are given to add from Table 4

Hindi primer for English speaking learners

491.43+864(T4)+21 English (T6) = 491.4386421

English readers for Hindi speaking readers

42+864 (T4) +9143(T6) = 428.649143

English readers for Hindi speaking Engineers

428.649143+024(As under-8642-8649, T4)+ 62 (from 001-999) =428.64914302462

Bilingual Dictionaries

The DDC is able to provide precise class numbers for bilingual dictionaries. Here the language in which the words are given make the base number; to the base from 420-490 is added the digit-3 (from Table 4), which means dictionaries, to the result is added the language number from Table 6 for the language in which meanings are given as taken. Thus the formula is:

Base number+3 (Table 4) +second language (Table 6)

For example, take Sanskrit-German Dictionary. Here Sanskrit forms the base number, as the entry words are given in Sanskrit.

491.2+3+31, the number for German from Table 6

=491.2+3+31=491.2331

Similarly, the class number for a

German-Sanskrit dictionary will be

43+3+912=433.912

(Here 43 is the base number for German and 912 the number for Sanskrit as taken from Table 6.)

Similarly:

Russian-Punjabi dictionary

491.7+3+9142=491.739142

English-French Dictionary

42+3+41=423.41

Table 4 may also be supplemented by Table 6 as already shown.

Use of English words in Hindi language.

It is a study of Hindi, so it will form the base number. For foreign elements we have 24 in Table 4 which is further extendable by Table 6:

491.43+24(T4)+21, the number for English from Table 6

=491. 43+24(T4)+21(T6)=491.432421

Similarly,

French phrases in the English language

42+24+41=422.441

Dictionary of French phrases in English Language

422.44103

It may further be noted that in the schedule of Main Class 400 Languages class numbers for all the known languages do not exist. But the base number for such unenumerated languages can be crystallised through the use of Table 6. Instructions to add from Table 6 exist in such cases. For example:

Tocharian Language

The class number for it has not been given specifically. At 491.9, we have Baltic and other languages. Some languages have been enumerated; 491.99 is for other languages. Instructions say that to obtain the class number for other languages, we are to add to 491.99 the number following 9199 in 91991-91998 from Table 6. There the number for Tocharian is: 91994.

Thus the number for Tocharian is:

491.99+4=491.994

Similarly, let us have the number for Egyptian (It belongs to the family of Non-Semitic Afro-Asian languages whose class number is 493). As per instructions at 493, the class number for Egyptian is:

493+1(from931 (T6)) =493.1

Similarly for Mongolic languages (which belong to the Ural-Altaic languages family (from 9423 (T6)) the base number is 494. The class number thus is:

494+23(from 9423(T6)) =494.23

Some other class numbers illustrating the use of Main Class 400:

American English

427.9+73(T2) =427.973

Indian English

427.9+54(T2) =427.954

Pakistani English

427.95491

(In the above two examples, 427.9 has been subdivided

by the area table.)

English dialect of London

427.9+421(T2) (from 421 London T2) = 427.9421

West Sussex dialect of English

427.9+4226(T2) =427.94226

9

Use of Table 5: Ethnic and National Groups

This table enumerates people based upon their, ethnic, or national origin. In the 18th edition, the use of this table was very limited as it could be used only on invitation, but since the 19th edition, its application has been universalized through the ss 089. It means that a subject can be treated with respect to groups of people characterized by their national, or ethnic origin, even if there are no instructions in the schedules to add from Table 5. Its use is simple: where there are instructions in the Schedules, we are simply to add the appropriate notation from Table 5 to the designated base number.

Psychology of the Dutch ethnic groups.

For the psychology of specific ethnic groups, we have the class number

155.84

Under this class number, we have instructions that to the-base number 155.84 add the number from Table 5, where the number for the Dutch is 3931. The full class number therefore is :

155.84+3931 = 155.843931

Similarly, psychology of Danish ethnic groups

155.84+3981=155.843981

Class numbers for some of the lesser known religions are obtainable with the application of Table 5:

299 Religions of other origin

299.92 Religions of other ethnic origins (vol. 2, p. 323)

Here we are instructed to add to the above base the number following 99 in 991-999 from Table 5

Religion of Polynesians

299.92 + 4 (from 994 T5) = 299.924

Religion of Khmer people (a religion founded in Southeast Asia)

299.5 + 932 (from 95932(T5)) = 299.5932

Druidism (a religion of the Celts)

299+16(from 916,T5) =299.16

Another officially invited use occurs at 305.81-.89. Sociology of Ethnic and national social groups:

A social study of Bengalis

(Bengalis are a linguistic-ethnic group)

305.8 is the base number to which the notation for Bengalis is to be added from Table 5 as per instructions:

305.8+9144(T5)=305.89144

Sociology of Bengali Women

305.48(from 305.486-.488) +8(from 305.6-305.8)
+ 9144(T5,Bengalis)

=305.4889144

Social study of Bengalis women In Bangladesh

305.4889144+09+5492(T2)=305.4889144095492

Jewish society [Secular aspects]

305.8+924=305.8924

Sociology of Jews in Germany

305.89240943

Another inevitable use of Table 5 occurs at 641.592 Ethnic cooking. Here instructions exist to add to the above base the notation from Table 5 for the cookery of ethnic groups.

Punjabi cooking

641.592+91421=641.59291421

Punjabi-Canadian Cooking

641.59291421071

Kashmiri cooking

641.592+91499 (T5) = 641.59291499

Another official use of Table 5 is made at 789.21-.29 Music of ethnic and cultural groups. (In DDC23 the class 789 is optional)

Folk music of Punjabis

789.2+9142=789.29142

Folk music of Pashtuns (Afghans)

789.2+91593(T5)=789.291593

Folk music of the Dutch

789.2+3931=789.23931

As given under 789.21-.29 (v3:714) the number extended by Table 5 can be further specified by a series of special subdivisions

History of folk music of Punjabis

789.291421+009=789.291421009

General principles of folk music of Punjabis

789.291421+01 =789.29142101

Instruments of Punjabi folk music

789.291421+02=789.29142102

Flute in Punjabi folk music

789.291421+02+83 (from 788.3)

=789.2914210283

Punjabi folk music in England

789.291421+0+42 (Table 2)

= 789.291421042

Some of the numbers in Table 5 are further divisible by Table 2. For example, the subdivision -68 Spanish Americans is further divisible by national groups of Spanish Americans by the addition of notation 7-8 from Table 2 to the base number -68.

Colombian people-68(T5)+861(T2) = -68861

Bolivians

- 68(T5)+84(T2) = -6884

Therefore, the class number for folk music of Bolivians is:

789.2+6884=789.26884

Similarly, national groups of Arabs are obtainable by the addition of area notation 5-6 from Table 2 to the base number-927(T5).

Libyans

927(T5)+612(T2) = -927612(T5)

Therefore, the class number for Libyan society is:

305.8+927612=305.8927612

Libyan in the US- a social study

305.892762073

Occasionally the area from Table 2 is added through the addition of zero as a facet indicator e.g. -96073 United States Blacks. For US Blacks in Canada the notation may be obtained by adding the area number for Canada to the above base, but through the addition of a zero, (see instructions at 96073 Table 5), e.g.:

- 96073071

Indians in the US

- 91411073

Bengalis in England

-9144+0+42(T2) = -9144042

Brazilians in the USA

-698+0+73(T2) = -698073

Nepalis in India

-91495+0+54(T2) = -91495054

Let us use the above synthesized table numbers into full class numbers:

Social study of Indians in the United States.

Here Indians are a national group.

The base class number is 305.8. As per instruction, to this base the number for Indians is added from Table 5.

Social study of Indians

305.8 as given under 305.81-.89 + 91411

= 305.891411

For "Indians in the USA" to the resultant class number add 0 and then the area number for the USA as taken from Table 2.

305.891411+0+73 (Table 2)=305.891411073

Similarly:

Social study of Nepalis in India

305.8+91495054=305.891495054

Folk music of Libyans

789.2(from 789.21-29)+927612 (Table 5) =789.2927612

Folk music of Libyan in Europe

789.292761204

History of Jews throughout the world

909.04+924 (From Table 5)=909.04924

Similarly:

History of Punjabis in the world

909.04+91421=909.0491421

Period subdivisions of world history as given under 909.1-909.8 can also be added with a zero as facet indicator.

World history of Punjabis in the 19th century.

909.04+91421 (Table 5)+0+81(909.81) =909.0491421081

World history of Celts in the 20th century

909.04+916 (Table 5)+0+82=909.04916082

Collected biographies of Jews

920.0092+924 (Table 5) = 920.0092924

Collected biographies of Punjabis

920.0092(from 920.0092-00929)+91421(Table 5)=920.009291421

Collected biographies of Celts

920.0092+916 (Table 5)=920.0092916

Education of Punjabis in Canada

Education of specific kinds of students 371.82

Students by nationality 9

(As per instruction we have to add to 371.82 the number following-08 in 081-089 (Table 1). There the number for Ethnic groups is 089.)

Punjabis (as-089(T1)) 91421(T5)
is further divisible by T5

in Canada as per instruction in T5 0+71

371.82991421071

Education of Eskimos in the USA

371.829+971 (Table 5)+073=371.829971073

Sinhalese migrant labour in New York State

331.63+9148 (Table 5)+0+747 (Table 2)

=331.6391480747

Use of Table 5 through the standard subdivision - 089

Apart from a few officially recognised situations demanding the use of Table 5, this table can also be used anywhere through the use of ss 089:

Child labour among Indians

331.31+089 (Table 1)+91411 (Table 5)

=331.3108991411

Papier-mâché among Kashmiris in England

745.542+089+91499+0+42=745.54208991499042

(As per instruction T5,vol.1 p.691, Para 3)

Reading habits of Indians

028.9+089+91411=028.908991411

Reading habits of Indians in England

028.908991411 +0+42=028.908991411042

10

Use of Table 6: Languages

Whenever any subject is further divisible by a language facet, notation from Table 6 is added to the specified base number. Provision of a separate table listing almost all languages has made possible the detailed enumeration of many lesser known languages not hitherto easy to identify.

Table 6 is to be used to supplement any number from the Schedules or even from the Tables (only on invitation). For example, the division of general encyclopaedias has been on broad language groups, which can further be sorted into individual languages by the use of Table 6:

036 Encyclopaedias in Spanish and Portuguese

For any specific language encyclopaedia in this language group, one has to add to 03 the number for the particular language in 61-69 in Table 6, as per instructions:

Spanish encyclopaedias

036+1(from 61, T6) = 036.1

Research in Spanish encyclopaedias

036.1+072 (As under 031-039)= 036.1072

Encyclopaedias in Galician

036+99(from 699, T6) = 036.99

Similarly, 039 is encyclopaedias in other languages (not provided for in 031-038). Class numbers for other encyclopaedias in other languages are to be obtained by adding language notation 7-9 from Table 6 to base number 039.

Vishv Kosh (Encyclopaedia in Hindi)

039+9143(T6)=039.9143

Encyclopaedic book of miscellaneous facts in Hindi

039.9143+02=039.914302

Similarly, class numbers for various translations of the Bible are also got by the use of Table 6:

220.5 Modern versions and translations [of the Bible]

220.53-.59 in other languages.

For languages other than English we are asked to add the number for the corresponding language from Table 6 to the specified base 220.5:

The Bible in Hindi

220.5+9143 = 220.59143

The Bible in German

220.5+31=220.531

Concordance to Bible in German

220.531+3(As under 220.5201-5209 vol. 2: 183) =220.5313

Vedic literature in English

294.5921+045 (as under 294.592, v2:280) + 21 (T6 as under 045)

= 294.592104521

Translation of Ramayana in French

294.5922+045+41=294.592204541

Though Table 6 has been used at a fairly large number

of places in the Schedules, main Classes 400 Languages and 800 Literature appear to be the home fields of its applications. In these two fields, the use of this table has already been discussed and illustrated while dealing with the use of Tables 3 and Table 4 respectively.

In Main Class 400 Languages (vol. 2) all the major languages have been enumerated with the exception of some lesser known languages. But Table 6 contains an almost exhaustive list of all known languages. Therefore, class numbers for these unenumerated languages can be obtained by the use of Table 6 on instructions.

For example:

470	Latin and Italic Languages
479	Other Italic Languages

to be obtained by adding to the base number 479 the number following 79 in 794-799 in Table 6.

Study of Faliscan language

Faliscan language is one of the Italic languages, which has not been enumerated under 470-478. Therefore, it will obviously go to 479. In Table 6 under 79 and its parts, we see that the notation for Faliscan is 794. Following the instructions, the class number for Faliscan is:

479+4 (from 794 of Table 6)=479.4

(We have added to 479 the digits following 79, which is 4).

Similar instructions appear at 491.99,493,494,495.92-97, 496.33,496.391-.399,497,498 and 499.

Here class numbers for some of the languages have been constructed as per instruction.

Again, take the Tupi language (a South American native language). Its class number is:

498+3832 [from 983832(T6) = 498.3832

This number is also given readymade

As per instructions under class number 498 notation from T4 can be added to the thus arrived number. For example

Grammar of Tupi

498+3832+5(T4) = 498.38325

Tupi English dictionary

498.3832+3(T4)+21 (T6) = 498.3832321

The use of Table 6 in conjunction with Table 4 for bilingual dictionaries in 400 has already been demonstrated in the chapter on the use of Table 4.

In the 800 Literature schedule some of the non-enumerated languages can be obtained by the use of Table 6. The use here is similar to its use in 400 languages.

For example, 893 Non-Semitic Afro-Asiatic literature

(Here the particular literature in this family of languages is to be obtained by adding to the base number 893 the numbers following 93 in 931-937 from Table 6.) Of Course numbers for some languages have been given readymade as illustrations.

Egyptian literature

893+1(from931(T6))=893.1*

(Since 931 is Egyptian in Table 6.)

Similarly:

Somali literature

893+54(from 9354(T6)) = 893.54*

Somali Epic poetry

893.54+1032 (T3B)=893.541032

History of Egyptian poetry

893.1+1009(T3B)=893.11009

Another use of Table 6 is at 372.65

Foreign or second languages in elementary schools.

The teaching of specific foreign or second languages in elementary schools is got by adding to the base 372.65 the relevant notation 2-9 from Table 6.

Hindi as a second language in elementary schools

372.65+9143(T6)=372.659143

German as a foreign language in elementary schools

372.65+31(T6)=372.6531

Class numbers derived from 372.65 can further be synthesised by adding special facets enumerated under 372.652-659(p. 842, vol.2)

Curriculum in German as a second language in elementary schools

372.6531+043=372.6531043

Methods for Teaching German as a second language in elementary schools

372.6531+044=372.6531044

Method of teaching English as second language in Primary Schools of India

372.65+21(T6)+044 + 09 (T1) + 54 (T2)

= 372.65210440954

Some more examples:

A general periodical in Hindi

059+9143=059.9143

A general periodical in Romanian

055+91(from 591(T6)) =055.91

A general periodical in Spanish

056+1(from6l (T6))=056.1

A French encyclopaedia

034+1 (from 41 (T6)) = 034.1

Dictionary of French encyclopaedias

034.103

English proverbs

398.9+21=398.921

Spanish proverbs

398.9+61=398.961

Hindi proverbs

398.9+9143=398.99143

Sanskrit calligraphy

745.6199+12 (from 912 (T6)) = 745.619912

English-French dictionary

42+3(Table 4) + 41 (Table 6) = 423.41

For more examples go back to the use of Table 4, Chapter 8.

11

Groups of People

This chapter deals with classification of subjects involving persons by their social, psychological, or other individual characteristics, such as health, age, marital status, and profession. This is done through the use of the ss-08 in Table 1 or by making use of the add to ... instruction from the schedules mostly through 011 - 999. For example, take

Baptists as social groups.

It is a subject of sociology, where social groups are placed at 305, and here the social stratification of various religious groups is placed under 305.6. Here as per instructions, we are to add to the base 305.6 the number following 2 in 230-299 in the Schedules. The notation for Baptists is 286, so we will add 86 to the designated base:

305.6+86=305.686

is the appropriate class number.

A social study of Indian Baptists

305.6+861(A under 286.14-.19) + 54(T2)

= 305.686154

Another such invitation is extended at 390.4 Customs of

people by occupations. It is to be further subdivided by 001-999. For example:

Social customs of artists

390.4+7(from 700)=390.47

Social customs of Painters

390.475

Customs of lawyers

390.4+34(from 340) =390.434

Similarly, 704 Special topics in the fine and decorative arts can be studied in respect of groups of people from 03 to 08 as under 704.03-704.08.

Child artists

704.08+3(from T1-083)=704.083

Art works by scientists

704.08+8(from 088 T1) + 5 (for scientists from 001-999) =704.0885

Jew artists

704.08+9(from-089 T1)+924(T5)

=704.089924

Directory of Jew artists

704.089924+025(T1)

=704.089924025

Directory of Jew artists of USA

704.089924025+73(T2)

=704.08992402573

174 is Economic, professional, occupational ethics. Ethics of some of the professions have been enumerated, e.g.:

174.2	Medical professions
174.3	Legal professions

Ethics for all other professions have been placed at 174.9, and we have been asked to get the individual class number for ethics of rest of the professions by adding notation from 001-999 Schedules. For example:

Ethics of librarianship

174.9+02(from 020 in 001-999)=174.902

In addition to its invited use at various places in the schedules, the use of a discipline by specified persons has also been suggested in various auxiliary tables. For instance, in Table 1 (Standard subdivisions) 024 Works for specific types of users is further extendable by 001-999 for works specifying the type of user:

Library classification for philosophers

025.42 is classification. For a subject meant for a specific type of user, we have the ss 024, which as per instructions is further divisible by 001-999. For philosophers we have the notation 100 in the schedules. Thus the complete class number is:

025.42+024(T1) +1 (from 001-999)=025.420241

Philosophy for librarians

100+024 (Table 1) + 020 (from 001-999)

=100+024+02=102.402

Similarly:

Mathematics for engineers =Mathematics for a specific type of user

51+024=510.24

For engineers, we have notation 620 from the schedules, vol. 3

So the complete class number is

510.24+62=510.2462

In such cases, it is essential to differentiate between a subject by a specific group of people and for a specific group of users.

In T2 the Area Table, 176 denotes regions where specific Religions predominate. Here 176 has been further divided on the basis of some enumerated religions, while all the other unenumerated religions have been placed at 1762-1769, and we are asked to add to 176 the number following 29 in 292-299 in the schedules.

For example, take "Islamic Regions of the World". As per the above instructions, we will add to the base 176 the number following 29 in 292-299, where the number for Islam is 297. Thus the desired notation for the above area is:

-176+7=-1767

Similarly countries where Buddhism prevails is

-176+43 (from 294.3) = -17643

If, say, our title is "Libraries in Islamic Countries of the World, we will proceed as follows

General libraries

027

For geographical treatment, we are to add to 027.0 (as the base) the area notation for the specified region from Table 2. The number for Islamic regions as already worked out is 1767. So, the appropriate class number is:

027.0+1767=027.01767

Wages in Islamic countries

331.29+1767=331.291767

Banking system in Islamic countries

332.1+091(T1) +767(from 1767) =332.1091767

Political situation in Buddhist countries

320.91+7643=320.917643

To all the subdivisions of notation 1 in Area Table 2 can be added all the subdivisions 3-9 of the Area Table through the facet indicator 0, as prescribed under -1(T2)vol. 1, p. 212. "Islamic countries of Europe" will be :

- 176(T2) +7(from 297)+0+4(T2)= -176704

Similarly:

Buddhist countries of Asia is

-176(T2) +43 (from 294.3 of schedule) + 0 +5(T2)

= -1764305

Therefore:

Libraries in Buddhist countries of Asia, is:

027.0+1764305=027.01764305

Libraries in Islamic countries of Asia

027.0+176(T2) +7(from 297) + 0 + 5(T2)

= 027.0176705

Political conditions in Buddhist countries of Asia

320.9+1764305=320.91764305

Groups of people also occur in Table 3C. There 352 is specific groups of people as a subject or theme of literature. As per instructions under-352 (in Table 3C) it is further subdivided by the notation 081-087 from Table 1. Further - 3529(T3C) is divisible by notations 05-09 and 1-9 from Table 5.

Treatment of women in literature

-352(T3C)+2(from 082,T1)=-3522

(it is different from literature for and by groups of people-8-9(T3C))

Similarly :

Portrayals of grandparents in literature

-352+53 (from 0853, T1) =-35253

Let us transform the above numbers into complete examples:

Collection of English poetry depicting women

82+10080 (T3B) +notation from Table 3C

=82+10080+3522=821.00803522

Portrayal of grandparents in English literature

82+080+35253

=820.8035253

Another use of persons in Table 3C occurs at 92 Literature for and by groups of specific people. As per instruction at 92 in T3C; we are to add to -920 notation 085-087 from T1 or to - 921 any number 001-999 from schedules

Collection of recent Urdu poetry by mathematicians.

Urdu Literature	891.439
poetry	1
modern period	71
(71 being taken from the period table at 891.4)	
collections, Table 3B	080 (from 100801-100809)
by specific kinds of persons (Table 3C)	921
by mathematicians from 001-999	51

891.439+1+71+080+921+51

=891.43917108092151

Similarly:

Critical appraisal of Hindi poetry composed by physically disabled poets (no period)

891.43+1009(T3B, vol. 1, p. 650) + 920(from 9205-9207,T3C)+ 7

=891.4310099207

Critical appraisal of late 20th century Hindi drama written by blind dramatists

891.43+2+71(Period)+09(from 1009 T3 B)+352(T3C) +920 (from 9205-9207,T3C) +71(from 0871,T1)

=891.432710992071

(Here 2 is drama from Table 3

71 is period from another special period table (v3:832)

09 as given under -1009 (T3B)

920 (from 9205-9207,T3C)

7 (from 087,T1)

Collection of recent Urdu poetry composed by women

891.439+1(T3B)+72 (Period from (891.4)+080 (from 10080,T3B)+9287 (women,T3C)

=891.4391720809287

An anthology of English poetry composed by poets of African descent in UK (no period)

82+10080(from - 100801-10809, T3B, Vol. 1, p. 650) + 8 (from 81-89,T3C)+96 (Africans,T5) + 041(UK)

=821.0080896041

Critical Study of Hindi Poetry by Dalits

891.43+1009(T3B)+920(T3C) +694(from 08694 T1) = 891.431009920694

Art works by scientists

704.08+8(from 088, T1) + 5 (for scientists from 001-999 as instructed under 088,T1)

= 704.0885

12

Examples Illustrating Multiple Synthesis

Multiple synthesis is defined as number building process by adding notations, to a given base number, taken from more than one place.

Liver diseases

616.362

Acupressure therapy for liver diseases

616.362+06(Therapy as under 616.1-616.9)+222 (from 615.8222)

=616.36206222

Domestic dogs

636.7

Veterinary medicine for domestic dogs

It will fall under

636.701-636.708 (p. 341, vol. 3)

As per instructions, we are to add to the base 636.70 the numbers following 636.0 in 636.01-636.08. There veterinary medicine is 636.089. So, we will add to 636.70 the number following:

636.0, i.e., 89

Hence the number is:

636.70+89=636.7089

Dog anatomy

Domestic animal anatomy is a subject of veterinary medicine, so we will first reach the above number as before:

636.7089

To arrive at the number for anatomy of dogs, now as per instructions we will add to 636.089 the number following 61 in 610-619: where anatomy is 611, thus we will add 1.

Dog anatomy is

636.7089+1 (from 611 as instructed under 636.089)

= 636.70891

The anatomy of the lungs of dogs

636.7089+124(from 611.24)=636.7089124

Encyclopaedia of the anatomy of the dog

636.7089+1003 (from 611.003) = 636.70891003

Note that the class number for an encyclopaedia of anatomy is

611.003.

Blood cancer in dogs

Dogs in animal husbandry 636.7

General principles of the animal husbandry of dogs has been placed at

636.701-.708

Veterinary medicine of dogs

630.70+89=636.7089

For specific aspects of veterinary medicine, we will add to 089, the numbers following 61 in 610-619 where blood cancer is 616.99418. Hence, we will add the number following 61, viz., 699418 to the above number. Hence,

636.7089+699418=636.7089699418

But if it is the Bone cancer in dogs, we will have to synthesize 616.994 [616.9942-616.9949] by the appropriate division of 611 where bone is 611.71

Hence the complete class number is:

636.7089+6994+71=636.7089699471

To repeat: Bone cancer in dogs

Dogs = 636.7

specific topics in dog husbandry = 636.701-.708

Base number for dogs husbandry = 636.70

Veterinary medicine of dogs = 89 (from 636.089)

Cancer = 6994 (from 616.994)

Bones (organs under 616.9942-.9949) = 71 (from 611.71)

636.7089699471

The following chart will further illustrate:

Animal husbandry 636	Animal husbandry of horses 636.1	Animal husbandry of dogs 636.7
Veterinary medicine 636.089	Veterinary medicine of horses 636.10+89=636.1089	Veterinary medicine of horses 636.70+89=636.7089
Veterinary anatomy 636.089+1=636.0891	(Veterinary) anatomy of horses 636.1089+1=636.10891	(Veterinary) anatomy of dogs 636.7089+1=636.70891
Veterinary anatomy of lungs 636.089+124=636.089124	Anatomy of horses lungs 636.1+089+124 =636.1089124	Anatomy of dogs lungs 636.7+089+124= 636.7089124

Similarly:

Lung cancer in horses

636.10 + 89 + 6994 (from 616.994) + 24 (from 611.24)

= 636.1089699424

Intestine cancer in cattle

636.20+89 (from 636.089)+ 6994 (from 616.994)+34 (from 611.34) =636.2089699434

Tuberculosis in cattle

636.20+89+6995=636.20896995

Bone tuberculosis in cattle

636.20+89+6995+71=636.2089699571

X-ray diagnosis of lung tuberculosis in horses

636.10+89+6995+24+07+572

=636.108969952407572

It is explained as below:

636.10	Animal husbandry of horses—Base number
89	Veterinary medicine (form 636.089)
6995	The number following 61 in 610-619 where number for TB is 616.995
24	Lungs: under 616.995 there is instruction to add to base 616.995, the number following 611 in 611.2-611.9, where class number for lungs is 611.24
07.	Pathology; added as instructed under 616.1-616.9 (p. 86,vol. 3)
572	X-ray diagnosis; we are asked to add to 07 the number following 616.07 in 616.071-616.079 where 616.07572 is X-ray diagnosis.

Some more examples of multiple synthesis:

Administration of a science library

Administration of a specific type of library 025.19 (Here, we have been instructed to add to the above base the number following 02 in 026-027, and the number for libraries devoted to a specific subject is 026, hence we will add 6. The class number 026 is further subdivided like 001-999, and the number for science is 500

Hence the class number is: 025.19 + 6 + 5 = 025.1965

Similarly:

Administration of special libraries on Indian history

025.19+6+954=025.196954

Administration of public libraries in India

025.19+74(from027.4)+54(T2)=025.197454

Rajya Sabha (Upper House of the Indian Parliament)

Legislative bodies have been placed at 328, which is to be subdivided by areas given under 328.4-.9

328+54(T2)=328.54 Indian parliament

Now, as per instructions under 328.4-.9, we are to add the special subdivisions enumerated there; houses of parliament fall under the subdivision 07, which is further to be subdivided like 328.31-328.39, the class number for an upper house is 328.31. Hence, we will add 1 to 07, and then will add this result 071 to 328.54, the complete class number being:

328+54+07+1=328.54071

Similarly:

Financial powers of the US Senate

328.73+07+412(from328.3412)=328.7307412

Again

331.124	Job vacancies [labour economics]
331.1242-.1249	Job vacancies in technological, manufacturing, agricultural, etc. occupations.

We are required to add to 331.124 numbers following 6 in 620-690.

Let us take:

Job opportunities in agriculture

331.124+30=331.1243

(The class number for agriculture is 630.)

Similarly:

Job opportunities in cotton agriculture

331.124+3351=331.1243351

The agriculture of cotton is 633.51, and we have added to the designated base the number following 6 in 633.51, viz, 3351).

Job opportunities in cotton storing

Since 633.51 is further extendable by 631.5, and the class number for cotton storing is

633.51+68=633.5168

Hence the complete class number for job opportunities in Cotton storing is:

331.124+3351+68=331.124335168

International law for trade in specific commodities

343.0871-.0875

For individualizing specific commodities, we are required to add to the base 343.087 the numbers following 381.4 in 381.41-.45.

For trade in agricultural commodities we have 381.41. So we will add 1, viz., the digit following 381.4 to the base number 343.087

343.087 + 1 = 343.0871

Not only this, the various agricultural products, can further be individualised by the digits following 63 in 633- 638.

International law of trade in Hashish

343.087 + 1 + 379 = 343.0871379

(As the class number for Hashish is 633.79 and we have added the digits following 63 in 633-638.)

Similarly:

International law of trade in coffee

343.087+1 (from 381.41) +373 (from 633.73 coffee)

= 343.0871373

Public administration in Communist countries

351.1 + 717 (from 1717 (T2)) = 351.1717

Public administration in communist Asian countries

351.1717+05=351.171705

Public administration in India

351 + 54(T2) = 351.54

Public administration in India : An encyclopedia

351+54(T2)+003(T1)=351.54003

Ministry of Finance of the Government of India

352.4 + 09 (T2) + 54 (T2) = 352.40954

President of the Republic of India

352.233 + 0(as under 352.3 - 352.6) +9 (from 093-099,under352-354) + 54 (T2) = 352.2330954

State administration in India

352.13 + 0 (as under 352.13 - 352.19) +9(from093-099,under352-354)+ 54 (T2) = 352.130954

Panchayati Raj system in India

352.17 + 09 (as under 352.13-352.19) + 54 (T2)

= 352.170954

Civil services system in India

352.63 + 0+9 (as above)+54 (T2)

=352.630954

As option A under 093-099 of 352-354 (p. 642, vol.2), the alternative number is:

351 + 54(T2) + 0 (as under 02-04 of 351.3-.9) + 263 (from 352.63) = 351.540263

Powers of the chief of civil services system in India: Powers of the UPSC Chairman

352.63+2 (from 22-26 under 352.2-352.6) +293 (from 352.293)+0+54 (T2) =352.632293054

Encyclopedia on the administration of justice

353.4+ 03 (T1) = 353.403

Administration of justice in India

353.4+09 (as under 352-354) + 54 (T2) = 353.40954

As Option A

351+54 (T2) +0 (as under 02-04 of 351.3-.9) + 34 (from 353.4) = 351.54034

Revenue administration in India

352.44 + 09 + 54 (T2)= 352.440954

Or

351+54 (T2) +0+244 (from 352.44) = 351.540244

Here we have followed the option A under 351.3-.9

Proposed budget of the Indian Government

352.48+ +0(from01-09 under 352.2-352.6)+954 (as under 093-099 of 352-354) = 352.480954

Budget for women welfare programmes in India

353.535 +0954(as under 352-354) = 353.5350954

Or

351+54(T2)+0(as under 02-04 of 351.3-.9)+3535(from 353.535)=351.5403535

Agriculture budget of India

354.5+2 (as under 22-26 under 352 -354) + 48 (from 352.48) + 54 (T2 as instructed above) + 01 (Special subdivision as under 352.493-.499)

= 354.52495401

Budget for social welfare programmes in India

353.5+2 (as under 22-26 of 352-354 (vol. 2, p. 625)) + 48 (from 352.48)+0 (from 01-09 under 352.2-352.6) + 954 (as under 352 - 354) = 353.52480954

Public administration of the economy in India

354+0954 (as under 093-099 of 352-354)

= 354.0954

Or

351+54 (T2) as instructed under 351.3-.9) + 0 (as under 02-04) +4 (from 354) = 351.5404

Ministry of home affairs of the Government of India

353.3 + 0954 (as under 093 - 099 of 352 - 354)

=353.30954

Or

351 + 54 (T2) + 0 + 33 (from 353.3) = 351.54033

Police services administration in Madhya Pradesh

353.36 + 09543 (for Madhya Pradesh)

=353.3609543

Or

351+543 (T2) + 0 + 336 (from 353.36) =351.5430336

Public administration of the postal services in India

354.759 + 0954 =354.7590954

or

351+54 (T2) + 0 + 4759 (from 354.759) 351.5404759

Government corruption in India

353.46 + 0954=353.460954

Or

351+54 (T2) + 0 + 346 (from 353.46) = 351.540346

Teaching methods for delinquent and problem students

371.93 + 3 (from 371.9043) = 371.933

Teaching problem students through educational games

371.93 + 3 (from 371.9043) + 37 (from 371.337) = 371.93337

Curriculum research in India

375.00072054

Curriculum in computer studies at primary level

372.34 + 043 (from under 372.8)= 372.34043

Government control of textbooks in India

379.1560954

Educational policy of India

379+54(T2) =379.54

Marketing management of E-mail services

384.34 + 0688 (T1) = 384.340688

Biophysics of mammals

571.4 *Biophysics

Here as per asterisked footnote we have been asked to add as instructed under 571 - 572 (p. 1129, vol. 2). Here we are to add to the base 571.4 the number following 571 in 571.1-571.2. The number for animals is 571.1. Hence we will add 1 to 571.4 i.e. 571.4 + 1 =571.41 Biophysics of Animals.

571.1 can be further subdivided by the number following 59 in 591-599. The number for mammals is 599. Hence we will further add 9 to make 571.41 + 9 = 571.419 Biophysics of Mammals.

Similarly, Effects of electricity on mammals

571.47 + 1 (from 571.1) + 9 (from 599 mammals)= 571.4719

Physiology of mammals

571.1 +9 (from 599) = 571.19

Physiology of primates

571.1 + 98 (from 599.8) = 571.198

Effect of cosmic rays on plants

571.459 + 2 (from 571.2 as under 571 - 572) = 571.4592

Effect of cosmic rays on Aquatic plants

571.459+2 (from 571.2 as under 571-572)+17 (from 581.7 from 581.71-76)+6 (from 577.6)= 571.4592176

Effect of electricity on cells

571.634+7(from 571.47)= 571.6347

Effect of electricity on Plant cells

571.634 cell biophysics +7 (from 571.47 electricity effects)+2 (from 571.2 as under 571-572,p.1129,vol.2)

=571.63472

Effect of electricity o cells of Bryophyte plants

571.63472 (as above) +8 (from 588 Bryophyte)

=571.634728

Effect of electricity on cells of Aquatic plants

571.634 cell biophysics +7(from 571.47, electric effect)+2 (Plants from 571.2, as under 571-572,p.1129, vol.2)+7(from 581.7 Plants of specific environment)+6 (from 577.6 Aquatic ecology)

=571.6347276

Ecology of the Indian Ocean area

577.7 + 5 (from 165 (T2)) = 577.75

Autoecology of the Indian Ocean area

577.7 + 5 + 0 + 26 (from 577.26 as instructed under 577.73 -.75) = 577.75026

A dictionary of bryophyte

588 + 03 (as instructed under 583 - 588, p. 1202 vol. 2) = 588.03

Study of genetics of bryophyte

588 + 1 (as under 583 - 588) + 35 (from 581.35) = 588.135

Museum on evolution of bryophyte

588+1+38(from 581.38)+074 (Museum as under 581) =588.138074

Genetics of worms

592.3 + 1 (as under 592 - 599) + 35 (from 591.35) = 592.3135

Models of the monkey brain

573.86 + 1 (under 573) + 98 (from 599.8 monkeys) + 0228 (TI, as under 592 - 599) = 573.861980228

Similarly:

Effect of high temperature on Dicotyledons

571.467+2(from 571.2 as instructed under 571-572, p. 1129, vol.2) +3 (Dicotyledons 583, as instructed under 571.21-.28) = 571.467 + 2 + 3 = 571.46723

Effect of high temperature on the seeds of the dicotyledons

571.467 + 2 + 3 (583 Dicotyledons) 1(as under 583-588)+ 467 (from 581.467 seeds) = 571.467231467

Similarly

Effect of ultraviolet radiations on Roses

571.456+2(Plants)+3734 (from 583.734 Roses) =571.45623734

Genetics of Gymnosperms

585+1 (as under 583-588, p. 1202, vol.2) +35(from 581.35 Genetics) =585.135

Evolution of Cryptogamia

586+1+38(from 581.38 Evolution) =586.138

Research on Evolution of Cryptogamia

586.138+072 (as under 581) =586.138072

Evolution of insects

595.7+1 (as instructed under 592-599 p. 1186, vol.2)+38 (from 591.38 Evolution) =595.7138

Genetic variation in Mollusca

594.1(as under 592-599)+35(from 591.35, Genetics)=594.135

Evolution of Cockroaches

595. 728+1(as under 592-599)+38 (from 591.38 Evolution) =595.728138

Synthetic organic drugs

615.31

We are asked to add to 615.31 the digits following 547.0 in 547.01-547.08 for specific synthetic drugs of organic nature.

For example:

Organometallic synthetic drugs

615.31+5=615.315

(As the number for organometallic compounds is 547.05, and we have added to the base 615.31 the digit following 547.0, viz.,5.)

This can be further synthesized to arrive at any specific organometallic drug: For example:

Organosodium synthetic drugs.

For organometallic drugs, we have 615.315, as above, under 547.05, we see that to obtain a class number for any specified organometallic compound, we have to add to 547.05 the digits following 546 in 546.3-546.7, the number for sodium in the above span is 546.382, so we will add 382 to the above worked out number.

615.315+382=615.315382

Similarly:

Organonickel synthetic drugs

615.31+5+625=615.315625

Organimetallic synthetic drugs of Nickel salts

615.315625+24 (salts, as under 546) =

615.31562524

Electrotherapy for heart diseases

For heart diseases, we have

616.12

The asterisk here leads us to the special subdivisions under 616.1-616.9 (on Vol. 3:84-88)

As per instructions, for therapy we add 06.

Thus for therapies for heart diseases we have

616.12+06=616.1206

But for specific therapies we have to add to 06 the digits following 615.8 in 615.82-615.89. Since the number for electrotherapy is 615.845, we will add 45 to the above.

616.12+06+45=616.120645 is the complete number

Similarly:

Electrotherapy for blood diseases

616.15+06+45 (from 615.845 Electrotherapy)

=616.150645

X-ray therapy for blood diseases

616.15+06+422 (from 615.8422 X-ray therapy)

=616.1506422

Pathology of female infertility

For female infertility we have

618.178

The asterisk here leads us to 618.1-618.8, where pathology is 07. Hence, the complete class number is:

618.178+07=618.17807

The subdivision 07 can be further subdivided like 616.075-616.079 if the aspect of pathology is specified.

Diagnosis of female infertility

618.178+07+5=618.178075

(We have added to 07 the digits following 616.07 in 606.077-606.079; as the number for diagnosis is 606.075 we have added 5.)

Similarly :

Diagnosis of diseases of pregnancy

618.3+07+5(from 616.075 Diagnosis) =618.3075
[This is also a readymade number]

Chemical diagnosis of pregnancy diseases

618.3+07+56(from 616.0756 Chemical diagnoses)

=618.30756

Animal pests of wheat

Here the agriculture of wheat is 633.11. The asterisk leads us to the instructions under 633-635 (v.3,p.307), and we are required to add 9 to the base number 633.11 for injuries, pests, and diseases. For specific kinds of injuries/ diseases/ pests we are asked further to divide the resulting number like

632.1-632.9. The number for animal pests is 632.6; so we will add 6 to the above. Hence,

633.11+9+6(from 632.6 Animal pests)=633.1196

Individual animal pests can be specified as instructed under 632.6. Let us say :

Monkeys as wheat pests

Wheat	633.11
Pests	9 (as under 633-635)
Animal pests	6 (from 632.6)

(We have added the digits following 632 in 632.1-632.9, and for animal pests the number is 632.6.)

Monkeys	98

(We have added to 6 the digits following 59 in 592-599, where the number for monkeys is 599.8.)

Hence the complete class number is

633.11 +9+6+98=633.119698

Similarly:

Rats as wheat pests

633.11+9+6+935=633.1196935

(The class number for rats is 599.35)

Rats as potato pests

635.21+9+6+935=635.2196935

Insect pests for grapes

Grape growing	634.8
Pests of Grapes	634.82

(We have been asked to add to the base number 634.82 the digits following 632 in 632.1-632.9, where the number for insect pests is 632.7. So, we will add 7, and the complete class number is 634.827

As per instructions under 632.7 we can individualize

the various insect pests: Say our title is:

Beetles as grape pests

Insect pests of grapes 634.82+7

To the above, we are to add the digits following 595.7 in 595.72-595.79. As the number for beetles is 595.76, we will add 6. Hence the complete class number is:

634.82+7+6=634.8276

Similarly:

Locust depredation of grapes

634.82 + 7(from 632.7 insect pests)

+ 26 (from 595.726 Locust) =634.82726

Bees as pests of oranges

634.31 +9+7+99(from 595.799 Bees) =634.319799

Bees as apple pests

634.11+9+7+99=634.119799

Applied physical chemistry (viz., application of physical chemistry in chemical technology).

660.29

For, specific aspects of applied physical chemistry, we are to divide the above number like 541.33-541.39. Let our title be

Applied photochemistry of specific radiations

660.29+53=660.2953

(The class number for photochemistry of specific radiations is 541.353. We have added to the base the digits following 541.3, viz., 53.)

Manufacture of equipment for shooting reptiles

Manufacture of equipment for hunting, fishing, and shooting has been placed at 688.79

We have been asked to divide this class number like 799.1-799.3, and shooting reptiles is 799.279.

Hence the complete class number is

688.79+279=688.79279

As per instructions under 799.279 class numbers for equipment for shooting individual kinds of reptiles can be individualized:

Manufacture of equipment for shooting crocodiles.

For reptiles shooting we have 688.79279. We have been asked at 799.279 to add further the digits following 597.9 in 597.92-597.98. So we will add 8 as the class number for crocodiles is 597.98. Hence

688.79+279+8=688.792798 is the complete class number. Similarly:

Equipment for shooting turtles (reptiles)

688.79+279(from 799.279 shooting reptiles) + 2 (from 597.92 Turtles) =688.792792

(The class number for turtles is 597.92.)

Manufacture of equipment for shooting Geese

688.79+244 (from 799.244 shooting water birds)+7 (598.417 Geese) =688.792447

(The class number for Geese is 598.417)

Manufacture of equipment for shooting turkeys

688.79+246 (from 799.246)+45 (from 598.645 Turkeys) =688.7924645

Flute music

788.32

Techniques for playing flute

788.32+1 (as under 784-788)+43(from 781.43) =788.32143

Dance music festivals in India

781.554+079 (As modified under 780.1-780.9) (from 01-09 as instructed under 781.2- 781.8) +54(T2) as under 780.79)

=781.55407954

Composition of dance music

781.554+1 +3 (from 781.3) =781.55413

Religious principles for the composition of Hindu sacred music

781.7+45 (from 294.5 Hinduism)+0+3312 (from 781.3312) =781.74503312

13

Classification of General Statistics, Law, Geography, and History

All these subjects have a common feature that the area, though taken from Table 2, is in fact a subject division, and usually occurs as an intervening facet instead of being the last one. It means the area notation is usually further extended by some subject division.

General Statistics 310.

The formula for general statistics, of specific countries and localities is:

31 (Base) +Area (fromT2)

General statistics of Asia

31+5(T2) =315

General statistics of India

31+54(T2) =315.4

General statistics of Gujarat

31+5475 (T2) =315.475

Law 340

Law has been first divided by its major branches preceded by international law:

341 Law of nations (International law)

342 Constitutional and administrative law

343 Military, tax, public finance, trade and industrial law

344 Labour, social, education and cultural law

345 Criminal law

346 Private law

347 [Civil] procedure and courts

348 Laws (Statutes), regulations, cases

349 Law of specific jurisdiction and areas

Then in the schedules each branch has been divided by the topic, and each topic under every branch begins with a zero:

344.01 Labour laws

344.02 Government-sponsored insurance laws

344.03 Social service laws

and so on.

But the preferred arrangement in the DDC is as follows.

The branch is first divided by the jurisdiction and then by the topic of law:

34X+area number+0X (i.e. 01-09) is the citation order:

(Where the first X stands for the branch of the law and the second for the subtopic of the corresponding branch.)

Let us say: Labour laws in India:

Labour Law, a division of 344 is 344.01. But as per the above citation order given under 344.3-.9 (p. 597, vol.2), we have

344+54(India from Table 2)+01 (topic: labour law) =344.5401

Obviously this citation order helps to bring together by

country all the subtopics of a branch of law:

Child Labour Law in India

344+54+01 (from 344.01)+31 (from 331.31)

=344.540131

Indian cases involving child Labour Law

344+54+01 (344.01)+31 (from 331.31)+ 0264 (cases, as under 342-347,p.557,vol.3)

=344.5401310264

Indian Law against Working of children in Tobacco industry

344+54+01+38 (from 331.38)+797 (from 679.7)

=344.540138797

Similarly:

Law of public health in India

344+54(T2)+04=344.5404

U.S. public health law

344+73 (from 344.04) +04 = 344.7304

Indian Law against (foetus) abortion

344+54(T2)+04192 = 344.5404192

Indian law for the control of AIDS

344+54(T2) +043 (from 344.043) + 69792 (from 616.9792 Aids) =344.5404369792

Library legislation in Punjab

344+54552+092=344.54552092

History of library legislation in Punjab

344.54552092+09(T1)

=344.5455209209

Supreme Court of India

347+54+035=347.54035

As per instructions, this can further be subdivided by

some special subdivisions enumerated under 347.02-347.04 (p. 621: vol. 2)

Judges of the Supreme Court of India.

347.54035+34=347.5403534

(34 is for judges as given under 347.02-347.04 p. 621 vol.2)

Court rules of the High court of Rajasthan

347+544(T2) +033 (from 347.033)+5(as given under 347.02-347.04)+1(from347.051) =347.54403351

Law of evidence in India

347+54+06=347.5406

Court decisions in law of witnesses in India

347.54+066+02643 = 347.5406602643

Indian marriage Law

346+54+016=346.54016

Court decisions on the marriage law in India

346 + 54 (T2) + 016 (from 346.016) + 02643 (as given under 342-347, p. 556-558, vol. 2) = 346.5401602643

There are also some other topics where subject subdivisions are added after the area. Take for example:

338.93-.99 Economic development and growth in specific continents, countries, localities

Economic policies of the USA

338.973

Economic subsidies in the USA

338.97302

(We have added to the base 338.973, a zero and the digits following 338.92 in 338.922-338.927 where 338.922 is subsidies.)

Theory and philosophy of economic subsidies in USA

338.97302+01 (from T1) =338.9730201

(The ss-01 has been added as instructed under 338.922)

Similarly:

Economic nationalisation policies of India

338.9+54(Table 2)+0+4(from 338.924)=338.95404

Communist parties in India

324.2+54(Table 2) +075 (subdivision under 324.24-.29)=324.254075

Conservative political parties in Pakistan

324.2549104

Rules and procedure of the US senate

328+73+05=328.7305

Debates in British Parliament

328+41 (Table 2)+02=328.4102

Financial powers of the Legislative Assembly of Tamil Nadu

328+5482(T2)+07(as under 328.4-.9)+412 (from 328.3412)

= 328.548207412

Geography and History

In the case of geography the formula is

91+area from T2+special subdivision (under 913-919, page v3:874-877)

Travels in Mughal India

91+54(Table 2)+04(page v3:875)+25(from 954.025) as instructed under 041-049 (p. 875, vol. 3)

=915.40425

Geography of the coastal regions of India

91+54(Table 2)+09 (page v3:877)+46 (from 146 of Table 2)

=915.40946

General geography of Christian-dominated areas of India

91+54+09+761 (from 1761 of Table 2)=915.409761

General geography of Muslim-dominated areas of Uttar Pradesh.

91+542+09+76 (from 176 of Table 2)+7(from 297 of schedules) =915.4209767

Travels in ancient China

91 +31 +04 (special subdivisions under 914-919) =913.104

Physical geography of ancient Macedonia

91+381+02=913.8102

Travels in the United States during Bill Clinton administration

91+73+04+929 (from 973.929)=917.304929

This number is also given as a readymade example

General geography of the forest regions of Texas

91+764+09 (special subdivision under 913-919)

+52(from 152 in Table 2) =917.640952

Geography of the Hilly regions of Greater Punjab of India

91+545+09+43 (from 143, T2)=915.450943

Similarly, the formula for History is:

9+(Area from Table 2)+Period subdivision from 930-990)

History of India

9+54=954

India under the reign of Emperor Akbar

9+54+0254(from 954.0254)=954.0254

History of Punjab

9+545 (from T 2) =954.5

History of Punjab during the reign of Akbar

9+545 (T 2) +0254 (from 954.0254) =954.50254

History of Jammu & Kashmir during the British Rule

9+546+03=954.603

History of islands of India

954+009 (from 0091-0098 under 930-990)+42 (from 142 (T2) Islands) = 954.00942

History of Christian regions in India

954+009+761 (from 1761 (T2)) = 954.009761

History of Muslim regions in India

954.009+176(T2) + 7 (from 297 Schedules) = 954.0091767

14

Exercises for Self Practice

(A) Use of standard subdivision

1. History of World Trade Organisation (WTO)
2. Journal of aptitude tests
3. Research in public administration in the U.K.
4. Chain store organization in Germany
5. Research in algebra
6. Research in algebra in ancient India
7. Jaipur Literature Festival
8. Indian trade catalogues of furniture
9. Directory of universities teaching journalism in Developing Countries
10. Journalism in the 19th century
11. Journalism in the U.K. in the 19th century
12. Journalism in the British colonies in the 19th century
13. Journalism in Muslim countries
14. Journalism in Muslim countries in the 19th century
15. Journalism in Portuguese-speaking areas of India
16. Journalism in Canada in the 19th century

17. Females in the media
18. Women journalists
19. Contributions of Pakistanis to media
20. Economic conditions in Muslim-dominated parts of India
21. Economic conditions in Christian-dominated parts of India
22. Economic conditions in India during 1947-1971
23. Political conditions in Non-aligned countries of Africa
24. Population density in Hindi-speaking areas of India
25. Rural development in India
26. History of the Third World
27. History of the Third World during Twenty first century
28. World history of the Communist bloc in 20th century
29. History of Christian nations since the 19th century
30. History of English-speaking nations

(B) Titles requiring the addition of two Areas from Table 2

31. Migration of people from India to the USA
32. Migration to the USA from poor countries
33. Migration of Buddhists to Europe
34. Exchange rate between the US dollar and the Indian rupee
35. Exchange rate between Communist currencies and the Euro
36. British colonies in Asia
37. British colonies in the Indian Ocean area
38. Artists in Muslim regions of India
39. Muslim artists
40. African American artists

41. African American (US Blacks) artists in New York
42. British financial investment in the Third World
43. Bangladeshi refugees in India
44. Sino-U.S. foreign relations
45. Foreign relations between U.S.A. and the Communist bloc
46. Foreign relations of Israel with Muslim countries
47. Foreign relations of Israel with Muslim countries of Asia
48. Foreign relations of India with British Commonwealth countries
49. Foreign relations of British Commonwealth countries of Asia
50. Labour workers from Nepal in India
51. Labour workers from Pakistan in the Middle East
52. India's economic assistance to Nepal
53. The U S economic aid to developing countries
54. Economic aid from British Commonwealth countries to poor nations
55. Russian economic aid to the Communist bloc in Europe
56. Trade between Japan and Canada
57. Trade between the Muslim nations and the Third World
58. Trade agreements between India and the U.S.A.
59. Trade agreements between Non-aligned nations
60. Public libraries in developing countries
61. Indian educational assistance to Nepal

(C) Illustrations Depicting Synthesis in the Schedules

62. Administration of university libraries
63. Administration of university libraries in India
64. Document selection in university libraries
65. Book selection in prison libraries

66. Book selection on international law
67. Book selection on the history of the U.S. Civil War (1861-1865)
68. Acquisition of publications from India by the US libraries
69. Selection and procurement of government publications
70. Acquisition of microforms in libraries
71. Problems of serials procurement in natural science in public libraries
72. Reference service in children libraries
73. Science journalism
74. Sports journalism
75. Aptitude tests for the medical profession
76. Aptitude tests for media
77. Psychology of deaf children
78. Emotions and feelings in animals
79. Astronomy as treated in the Bible
80. The Old Testament in Hindi
81. Historical books of the Old Testament in Hindi
82. The Ten Commandments in Hindi
83. Concordance of the Bible in Hindi
84. Doctrines of Eastern churches
85. Sacred shrines of Jains
86. Jain places of pilgrimages in Rajasthan
87. Job opportunities in documentation
88. Job opportunities in agriculture
89. Employment market for librarians.
90. Employment opportunities in agriculture
91. Compensation and conditions of employment in agricultural occupations

92. Wages of documentationlists
93. Wages in agricultural occupations in India
94. Trade unions of librarians
95. Agricultural workers union
96. Labour management disputes in documentation centres
97. Labour disputes of agriculture labour
98. Strikes by documentationlists
99. Strikes by agricultural workers
100. Economics of documentation cooperatives
101. Cooperative agriculture
102. Economics of poultry farming
103. Economics of metal extraction
104. Debates in Rashtriya Panchayat (Parliament) of Nepal
105. Social welfare services for cancer patients
106. Social welfare for persons suffering from lung cancer
107. Social welfare services in providing special diet to cancer patients
108. Residential care for alcoholics
109. Counseling for narcotics addicts
110. Social asylums for the mentally retarded
111. Providing shelter for flood victims
112. Teaching methods for slow learners
113. Lesson plans for teaching the mentally retarded
114. Corporal punishment in elementary schools in India
115. Use of TV in elementary schools
116. Science curriculum in elementary schools
117. Standards for laboratories in secondary schools of India
118. Teaching through audio-visuals in secondary schools in India

119. Teaching through audio-visuals in universities
120. Providing Midday meal to students in elementary schools
121. Folk tales about elephants
122. Folk tales about the intelligence of elephants
123. Folk tales about the medicinal value of roses
124. Satellites of the planet Saturn
125. Orbits of the satellites of the planet Saturn
126. Hindu chronological calendar
127. Acceleration of meson particles
128. Radio isotopes of radium
129. Thermo (Physical) chemistry of organic substances
130. Radioactive isotopes of organic substances
131. Radioactive isotopes of hydrocarbons
132. Radioactive isotopes of the aromatic hydrocarbons
133. Analytical biochemistry of plants
134. Biochemistry of cryptogamia
135. Biophysics of cryptogamia
136. Analytical biochemistry of cryptogamia
137. Journal of animal biochemistry
138. Analytical biochemistry of animals
139. Role of sugar in animal biochemistry
140. Function of proteins in animal biochemistry
141. Biochemistry of steroids (organic compounds) in invertebrates
142. Glucose in the biochemistry of insects
143. Biochemistry of eggs of insects
144. Analytical biochemistry of Orthoptera
145. Biochemistry of enzymes in Orthoptera
146. Regional physiology of the human head

147. Organometallic synthetic drugs
148. Synthetic organic drugs of sulfides
149. Synthetic organo-aluminum drugs
150. Synthetic organo-potassium drugs
151. Copper poisons
152. Lead salts poisons
153. Diagnosis of lung diseases
154. Ultra sound diagnosis of lung diseases
155. Spurious therapies of small pox
156. Mediaeval traditional remedies for diseases of bones
157. Activity therapy for arthritis
158. Climatotherapy for tuberculosis
159. Climatotherapy for tuberculosis of bones
160. X-ray diagnosis of bone tuberculosis
161. Rib fractures
162. Drug therapy for dental diseases
163. Electrotherapy for diseases of the gums
164. Case histories in children's diseases
165. Lighting in museums
166. Lighting in science museums
167. Energy conservative lighting in biological museums
168. Lighting in theaters
169. Lighting in hospital libraries
170. Concrete as a foundation material in civil engineering
171. X-Ray testing of concrete used as foundation material in buildings
172. Chemistry of agriculture
173. Physical chemistry of agriculture
174. Fertilizers for fruit orchards
175. Nitrate fertilizers for fruit orchards

176. Nitrate fertilizers for citrus fruits
177. Nitrate fertilizers for flower and ornamental plants
178. Poultry Feed
179. Snake farming (Snakes are reptiles)
180. Butterfly gardening
181. Snake farming in South India
182. Cereals foods
183. Home construction of raincoats for women
184. Rearing of delinquent and problem children
185. Home care for deaf children
186. Upbringing of Jewish children
187. Rearing of American Jewish children
188. Rearing of Canadian Punjabi children
189. Cost accounting in hospitals
190. Cost accounting in government offices
191. Audit reports of hospital accounts
192. Industrial production of nitrogen compounds
193. Industrial thermo chemistry
194. Industrial properties of Graphite coal
195. Pasteurization in the industrial production of wines
196. Journal of pottery technology
197. Research in pottery technology
198. Research in the U.S.A. in pottery technology
199. All-India Conference on pottery Technology
200. Industrial dyeing of silk
201. Industrial dying of polyester textiles
202. Industrial production of urea (fertilizer)
203. Industrial production of ammonium nitrate fertilizer
204. Physical metallurgy of brass

205. Physical metallurgy of nickel
206. Manufacture of ultraviolet spectroscopes
207. Material for manufacture of infra-red spectroscopes
208. Manufacturing of guitars
209. Manufacturing of instruments for maintenance and repair of pianos
210. Manufacture of field hockey sticks
211. Manufacture of equipment for ice skating
212. Installing air conditioning in museums
213. Installation of air conditioning in biological museums
214. Installing air conditioning in hospital libraries
215. Installing air conditioners in residential buildings
216. Air conditioning in residential Skyscrapers
217. Depiction of Buddhist themes in art works
218. Medical objects as art works
219. Use of steel in architectural constructions
220. Architecture of buildings for indoor games with special reference to handicapped persons
221. Architecture of multiple purpose auditoriums
222. Architecture of Hindu temples
223. Architecture of library science school buildings
224. Architecture of general library buildings
225. Architecture of hospital libraries
226. Remodeling of hospital libraries
227. Architecture of Bungalows for Solar Energy use
228. Effects of social conditions on the architecture of the National Library of India
229. Architecture of club houses for the aged people
230. Drawings of Indian landscapes
231. Drawings of penguins

232. Paintings depicting Indian history
233. Paintings on Indian Moughal history
234. Use of Computers in bird cinematography
235. Photographs of birds
236. Fishing for sharks
237. Sacred music of the Sikhs
238. Sikh sacred music for specific times
239. Orchestra music performances in London
240. A treatise on the recording of violin music.
241. World History of Sindhis in 20th century
242. Travels in the 19th century Punjab
243. Encyclopedia of the History of Goa

15

How to use the Relative Index

The Relative Index (RI) of the DDC23 comprising of 965 pages(37 pages larger than DDC 22) is contained in the fourth volume. It is an alphabetical key to the DDC schedules, tables, and the manual. Considered as innovative and everlasting contribution of Melvil Dewey to the science of library classification, it is an integral and aboriginal part of the Dewey's system – not merely an adjunct.

It is called relative as all the subjects scattered by discipline in the schedules are brought together in the Relative Index, and the relations between scattered but related concepts (distributed relatives) are displayed in the index. In the schedules due to division by discipline the different aspects of a subject get scattered. In the RI ingeniously these scattered relatives are brought together and displayed meaningfully showing relations of subordination, coordination, and of related terms. It means that in the index disciplines are subordinated to the subjects. In other words the RI easily relates a subject to its different disciplines.

The approach here is thus opposite to that of the schedules; and thus is complementary to access the system conceptually. Based on ISO 999:1996, *Guidelines for the content, organization and presentation of indexes*, it is an alphabetical list of all the:

a) headings, terms, concepts and notes appended to entries in the schedules (vols. 2-3);

b) terms in the six tables (vol. 1), Introduction and Glossary;

c) and broader concepts in the Manual (vol. 1).

Some concepts and terms implied and some terms obtainable through number building and having sufficient literary warrant have also been included in the index. Recognised synonyms of some of the terms (having sufficient literary warrant) have also been included to totally avoid see references except the see Manual at ... references. Apart from physiogeographic names and features, countries and their provinces are also included as in Table 2. Other categories of names included are of historical figures like kings, queens, eras, of heads of states, or regimes. Some schools of thought named after persons are there, though individually such persons have not been listed.

Each page of the RI has been divided into two columns by a vertical line in the centre. Each column consists of entries. An entry may be defined as a term or phrase followed by its DDC number on the right. An entry may (or may not) contain subentries, sub-subentries and "see also" and "see Manual at..." references. For example:

Pisacha languages	491.499
	T6-91499
Pisacha literatures	891.499
Pisces	597
Pisces (Zodiac)	133.5277

All entries are arranged word by word with first letter capital of the entry word.

Asia

Asia minor

Asian Americans

Asian flower arrangements

Asians

Asiatic

Subentries shown through indentions begin with a roman small unless it is a proper name:

Umpiring (Recreation)	790.1
American football	796.332 3
baseball	796.357 3
Canadian football	796.335 3
cricket	796.358 3
rugby	796.333 3
soccer	796.334 3
volleyball	796.325 3

Hyphen is treated as a space, i.e., a hyphenated word is treated as two words, e.g.:

Cross River

Cross-stich

Crossbills

Crossbreeding

or

PI (Macroeconomics)	
Pi-mesons	339.32
Pi-mesons	539.72162
Pi bas	787.82
Piecenza	T2-4546

Different punctuation marks are arranged as follows:

Term

Term. subheading

Term (Parenthetical qualifier)

Term, inverted part qualifier

Term as a phrase

For example

Canada

Canada. Parliament

Canada, Eastern

Canada, Western

Canada goose

Canadian Arctic

Central (Scotland)

Central Africa

or

Pisces	597
Pisces (Zodiac)	133.5277
United Nations	341.23
United Nations. Charter	341.232
United Nation. Economic... Council	34102325
United Nations. General Assembly	341.2322
United Nations. Security Council	341.2323
United Nations Children's Fund	362.7
United Nations Educational, Scientific, and Cultural Organisation	001.060.1
United Nations treaties Series	341.0262

American spellings have been used throughout

Catalogs	T1-0216
Catalogs (Bibliographic catalogs)	025.31

Labor

331

Labor (Obstetrics) 618.4

Initials and acronym are treated as a word and filed accordingly.

Ablutions

ABM (Missiles)

Aid to families....

AIDS (Disease)

Unemployment insurance

Unesco

Uneven bars(Gymnastic...)

Interestingly, initials and acronyms are entered both under the abbreviation and fully spelled form:

Military police (p. 543)	353.13323
MP (Military police (p.563)	353.13323
Value -added tax(p.914)	336.2714
VAT (Tax)(p.916)	336.2714
World Wide Web (p. 955)	004.678
WWW (p. 956)	004.678

Proper names beginning with numerals are filed before A, i.e., at the beginning of the RI:

35 mm cameras	771.32
100 Mile House (BC)	T2-71175
401 (k) plans	332.0240145
A level examination	378.1662
Aachen (Germany)	T2-435511

Proper names of all sorts are entered according to AACR2R (2002) specifications. Terminology is current and internationally used; American bias is being reduced gradually; commonly used forms of terms have been preferred. Plants and animals have been entered twice both under their taxomonomic and common names. Subjects denoted by a phrase are entered directly. It means that adjectival phrases begin with the adjective:

Agricultural banks
Agricultural credit
Agricultural libraries
Civil engineering
Civil engineers
Color television
Islamic calendar
Juda's betrayal of Jesus Christ
Pitman shorthand system

In some cases an adjectival phrase may be broken into a subentry to keep aspects of an important concept together:

India	954
	T2— 54
ancient	934
	T2— 34

But place names with directions are inverted, however:

Canada, Eastern	T2-713
Canada, Western	T2-712
England, Northern	T2-427

If the direction is a part of the name proper than it is not inverted:

North America	970
North Carolina	975.6
North Korea	951.93

The index is highly structured both semantically and typographically to yield maximum information while conserving space. Use of typographical indentions and syndetic device of "see also..." have skillfully been made to depict rank relations and reveal different aspects of the indexed subject . As shown earlier, an entry could be a stand alone, i.e., having no subentry or any see also... reference:

Dorset (England)	T2-4233
Double cropping	631.58
Double helix	572.8633

But many entries have subentries with related concepts beginning with a Roman small and listed alphabetically. For example (p. 701)

Public schools	371.01
finance	379.11
law	344.076
law	344.071
primary education	372.104 21
secondary education	373.224
see also Manual at 371 vs. 353.8, 371.2, 379	
Public schools (Private schools)	371.02
secondary education	373.222

The number 371.01 against the (unintended) main entry is the number for general/ comprehensive or interdisciplinary works on the subject of public schools. Some major aspects of public schools, namely Public schools finance, Law of public schools finance, and Public schools primary and secondary education have been listed alphabetically under the main entry "Public schools" leaving one indention to the right along with their respective class numbers. The term "law" given as subentry of the subentry finance means "Public schools finance law" has the class number 344.076, whereas the next entry of law means "Law of public schools" has the class number 344.071. Further the index users/

classifiers are advised to look under "Public education" for more or related topics on Public schools.

See also references are to relate broader or synonymous headings for wider choices. "See also..." references increase the recall ratio. Further for precise, compared and contrasted interpretation of Public schools the classifiers have been advised to look the *Manual* at some directed places. "See manual at..." notes, which are always given in italics, increase the precision ratio.

To repeat, when a topic treated from perspectives of two or more disciplines is represented by multiple numbers, the class number displayed on the index entry opposite the unintended (main) term is the class number for multidisciplinary/ comprehensive or general works on the subject. It is a suggestive number though this multi-disciplinary number is repeated under the discipline in which it falls. For example:

Olives	641.3463
agriculture	634.63
botany	583.87
commercial processing	664.80463
cooking	641.6463
food	641.3463

It simply means that all the interdisciplinary works on Olives are placed at 641.3463 though actually it is the number for Olive food. Since the DDC-21(1996) the provision of numbers for interdisciplinary subjects has been enormously increased.

Interdisciplinary numbers do not exist for all subjects for various reasons. In such cases the main entry having subentries is shown blank. For example,

Feudal Age	
European history	940.14

Japanese history	952.02

It simply means that there is no class number for interdisciplinary works on Feudal age.

How to consult the RI

The index is a list of single and multi-worded terms and phrases comprising of names of concepts, entities, persons, places, events, processes, etc., etc, all arranged in a single alphabetical word by word order. A single term is obviously looked into directly. If there is a recognised synonym of the term with sufficient literary warrant then the term is indexed under both; the less preferred term then also refers to the more preferred term with 'see also' reference where all other aspects of the subject are indexed as subentries. For example:

Internal commerce	381(p. 425)

It is a less preferred term for Domestic trade (p. 247)

Domestic trade	381
law	343.08
public administration	354.73

Domestic trade is a preferred term as it is a full entry with subentries

Going to the entry under Birds (p. 90-91):

Birds		598
agricultural pests		632.68
air transportation hazard		363.12412
animal husbandry		636.5
arts	T3C-	3628
commercial hunting		639.12
conservation technology		639.978
control technology		628.968
agriculture		632.68

disease carriers	571.986
medicine	614.434
drawing	743.68
paleozoology	568
resource economics	333.958
sports hunting	799.24
zoology	598

All the varied aspects of birds have been listed alphabetically while two aspects namely control technologies and disease carriers have their sub aspects, which may be termed as sub-sub-aspects of Birds.

For example, Birds as agricultural pests has the class number 632.68. Birds control technology has the class number 628.968. But for Birds control technology in/for agriculture has the class number 632.68.

In a multiword term having both concrete and abstract words, or words denoting an entity or process, we should look first under the concrete term or entity rather than the abstract or process word. For example, for

High seas law

Solar eclipse

Television transmission

Wetlands ecology

Zoology of dogs

We should look under High Seas, Solar, Television, Wetlands and Dogs respectively as these are the concrete entities in the above terms.

Similarly for Ancient India we should look under "India" as it is more concrete than the word ancient. If a term consists of equally concrete or abstract words then such a term may be indexed under both the words. For example "Insurance rates", appears as

Rates (Prices) (p. 716)

communication industry	384.041
insurance	368.011
transportation services	388.049

and also under Insurance rates 368.011 (p. 422). The term "Insurance rates" has a considerable literary warrant.

Since the 22nd edition in tune with the LC and Sears subject headings lists and the Library of Congress policies and in accordance with the current thinking in the profession in the days of online and networked information retrieval the adjectival phrases are entered directly, i.e., in uninverted form. For example:

Civil engineering	624
Commercial art	741.6
Engineering geology	624.151
Old Spanish language	467.01
Old Stone Age	930.12
Old World rabbit	599.322

In the previous editions these were entered as Engineering, civil; Art, commercial, and so on.

Terms from any of the six tables (in volume 1) or references to the *Manual* have been indicated so. Full forms of the standard and mnemonic abbreviations for the six tables along with other abbreviations used in the RI are given on page 3, volume 4:

TI	Table 1	Standard subdivisions
T6	Table 6	Languages

Other abbreviation pertain mostly to the states of the US and other places:

Rabun county (Ga)	T2-758123
Quoin (S. Aust.)	T2-94236

Here Ga. stands for Georgia State and S. Aust. stands for South Australia. In fact, since the RI of 21st edition (1996), unlike the previous editions, minimum use of abbreviations has been made.

It may be noted that the number from any of the tables are listed next to the interdisciplinary number/ or the number of the main entry. It is then followed by subentries (if any) in alphabetical sequence:

Forecasting	003.2
	T1- 0112
business	338.544
investment	332.678
management decision making	658.40355
marketing management	658.818
occultism	133.3
social change	303.49
weather	551.63

It means that class number for interdisciplinary works on forecasting is 003.2, and the term forecasting also appears in Table 1 Standard subdivisions at 0112. Rest of the aspects of forecasting have been listed alphabetically. Take another example.

India	954
	T2-54
ancient	934
	T2-34

The number for Indian history or interdisciplinary works on India is 954. India also occurs in Table 2 at 54. The number for Ancient India (subentry) is 934 and this term also occurs in Table 2 at 34.

For a reference to any entry or subentry in *Manual* there is a direct instruction to see Manual at... a particular reference:

Miniatures	688.1
	T1 -0228
Handicrafts	745.5928
see Manual at 745.5928	
manufacturing technology	688.1

The instruction *see Manual at..* always appears in italics. It is clear from the indention that *see Manual* at 745.5928 is a subentry of handicrafts and not of the main entry Miniatures. It means that for discussion/explanation of classification of miniature handicrafts the classifier should consult the manual at number 745.5928 (p. 141, vol. 1). Here there is a long note for different possible numbers for handcrafted miniatures and models. The manual provides relevant and free discussion about the topic for comparison and contrast with other related or seemingly similar topics and their class numbers. The *manual* provides information for better interpretation of an entry and helps in inter-indexer consistency. However since the DDC22 (2003) references to the manual have been reduced.

No index can be totally exhaustive, so is the Relative Index; index is not an alphabetical recapitulation of the schedules and tables. The categories of terms not included have been listed in Section *11.15* of the Introduction (p. lxx, vol. 1). These are "phrases beginning with the adjective form of countries, languages, nationalities, religions, e.g., English poetry, French cooking, Italian architecture, Hindu prayer books" . Exceptions are the cases with a strong literary warrant, e.g., English literature. If the name is a unique proper noun then it may be included, e.g., English Channel, Indian Ocean, Indian hemp., French bulldog. **Other category of excluded terms is the concepts divisible by standard subdivisions, e.g., Science dictionaries, Research in religions.**

If a concept is not found directly then its broader class may be looked for to arrive at some base number. For example, for a class number of Jawaharlal Nehru University we should look under universities; for a biography of Sachin Tendulkar we should look under cricket, where the appropriate term seems cricket players. As an another example, for Bahadur Shah Zafar, the last Mughal King, we should look under "Mughal Empire". As another example, for postal rates we should look under "Rates, communications industry"

The Relative index if properly operated brings alive many topics buried in the schedules. It is simple, smart and easy to use.

16

Answers to Exercises for Self Practice

(A) Use of standard subdivisions

1. 382.9209
2. 153.940005
3. 351.072041
4. 381.12+065 (as under 380) + 43 (T2 as under 065) = 381.1206543
5. 512.0072
6. 512.0072034
7. 800+074(T1)+54(T2)=807.454
8. 684.10029+54(T2) =684.1002954
9. 070.0711+1724(T2) =070.017111724
10. 070.09034
11. 072.09034
12. 079.17124109034
13. 079.1767
14. 079.176709034

15. 079+54 (Table 2) + 09175 (Table 1) + 69 (Table 6) = 079.540917569
16. 071.109034
17. 070+082(Table 1) =070.082
18. 070.4082
19. 070+089(Table 1)+914122(Table 5)=070.089914122
20. 330.9 + 54+009 (Table 1)+176(from Table 2)+7 (from 297 of schedules) = 330.9540091767
21. 330.9+54(T2)+009(ss TI)+1761 (T2)=330.9540091761
22. 330.9+54(T2) +04 (from 954.04)=330.95404
23. 320.960091716
24. 304.61+09(T1)+175(T2) +9143 (T6) +0 +54 (T2)= 304.61091759143054 (see option under -1 Areas in general (T2) p. 212, vol. 1)
25. 307.14+1 (as under 307.1-307.3) +2(from 307.72) + 09(T1) + 54 (T2) = 307.14120954
26. 909.09+724(from Table 2, from 1724)=909.09724
27. 909.09724+0+83(from909.83)=909.09724083
28. 909.09717082
29. 909.09+761(from 1761(T2))+0+8(from 909.8)= 909.0976108
30. 909.09+75(from l75(T2))+21(T6)=909.097521

(B) Titles requiring addition of two areas from Table 2

31. 304.8+73+0+54=304.873054

    Note that the country of destination is to be taken first and the place of origin comes as latter facet.
32. 304.8+73+0+1724=304.87301724
33. 304.8 +4(T2) +0+176 (T2) +43 (from 294.3) =304.84017643
34. 332.45609+73+0+54=332.4560973054
35. 332.456091 + 717 (from T1 - 1717) + 0 + 4 (T2)

=332.45609171704

36. 325.3+41+09+5(T2)=325.341095
37. 325.3+41+091(T1)+824(from 1824, T2)=325.341091824
38. 709.54091 + 76(from 176,T2) +7 (from 297 of schedules) = 709.54091767
39. 704.08+8(from 088 (Tl))+297 (schedules) = 704.088297
40. 704.03+96073(T5)=704.0396073
41. 704.03+96073(T5)+0+747(T2)=704.03960730747
42. 332.673+41+0+1724=332.6734101724
43. 325.2109+5492(T2)+0954=325.210954920954
44. 327+51+0+73=327.51073
45. 327.7301717
46. 327+5694(T2)+0+176(T2)+7(from 297 schedules) = 327.569401767
47. 327+5694(T2)+0+176(T2)+7(from297)+0+5(T2) = 327.56940176705

    (Third area facet has been added as per option under-1(T2) p. 212, vol. 1)
48. 327+54(Table 2)+0+1712(T2)+41(T 2) =327.540171241
49. 327.0917 124105
50. 331.62+5496+0+54=331.625496054
51. 331.62+5491 +0+56=331.625491056
52. 338.91+54+0+5496=338.915405496
53. 338.917301724
54. 338.911+712 (from 1712 (T2) +41(T2) + 0+ 1724 (T2) = 338.9117124101724
55. 38.91+47(T2)+0+1717(T2)+0+4(T2)=338.91470171704
56. 382.09+52+0+71=382.0952071
57. 382.091+76(from 176,T2)+7 (from 297 Islam)

=382.091767

58. 382.9+54(T2)+0+73(T2)=382.954073
59. 382.911+716(from 1716(T2))=382.911716
60. 027.4091724
61. 379.129+5496(T2)+0+54(T2)=379.1295496054

(C) Illustrations depicting synthesis in the Schedules

62. 025.19+77(from 027.7)=025.1977
63. 025.19+77(from 027.7)+54(T2)as under 027.7) =025.197754
64. 025.218+77(from 027.7)=025.21877
65. 025.218+7665 (from 027.665)=025.2187665
66. 025.27+341=025.27341
67. 025.27+973.7=025.279737
68. 025.29+54(T2)+0973=025.29540973
69. 025.28+34(from 025.3434)=025.2834
70. 025.28+94(from 025.3494)=025.2894
71. 025.27+5 (from 500)=025.275 (This is the officially preferred number)

    or

    025.28+32(from 025.3432)=025.2832
72. 025.527+7625 (from 027.625)=025.5277625
73. 070.449+500=070.4495
74. 070.449+796=070.449796
75. 153.94+610=153.9461
76. 153.94+070=153.9407
77. 155.45+12(digits following 371.9: The number for deaf children being 371.912)=155.4512
78. 156.2+4(from 152.1-152.8)=156.24
79. 220.8+52=220.852
80. 221+5(from 220.1-220.8)+9143 (Table 6) =221.59143

81. 222+0 (as instructed under 221-229)+5(from 220.5) + 9143(T6)=222.059143
82. 222.16+0+5+9143=222.16059143
83. 220.5+9143(T6)+03(as under 220.5201-.5209) =220.5914303
84. 230(as instructed under 230.1-.9)+15(from281-289 where Eastern churches are 281.5) =230.15
85. 294.4+35(from 203.5 as under 290 p. 273, vol.2) =294.435
86. 294.4+35+09544=294.43509544
87. 331.1241+025 (from schedules)=331.1241025
88. 331.124+30(from 630)=331.1243

    (We have added to the base 331.124, the digits following 6 in 620-690. The class number for agriculture is 630.)
89. 331.1291+020=331.129102
90. 331.129+30(from 630)=331.1293
91. 331.204+30=331.2043
92. 331.281+025=331.281025
93. 331.28+30+0954=331.2830954
94. 331.8811+020=331.881102
95. 331.881+30=331.8813
96. 331.89041+025=331.89041025
97. 331.8904+30=331.89043
98. 331.89281+025=331.89281025
99. 331.8928+30=331.89283.
100. 334.681+025=334.681025
101. 334.68+30=334.683
102. 338.17+65 (from 633-638, where poultry is 636.5) =338.1765
103. 338.27+4(from553.2-553.9)=338.274

104. 328.549602
105. 362.19+6994 (from 616-618)=362.196994
106. 362.19+6994+24 (from 611.2-611.9) =362.19699424
107. 362.19+6994 (from 616.994) +0+6(from 362.176) =362.19699406
108. 362.292+85 (from special sub-divisions under 362-363) =362.29285
109. 362.293 + 86(as under 362-363) = 362.29386
110. 362.3+85(as under 362-363)=362.385
111. 363.3493+83(as under 362-363)=363.349383
112. 371.926+3(from 371.9043-371.9047)=371.9263
113. 371.9280+3028(from 371.9043028)=371.92803028
114. 372.1+542(from 371.542)+0954 =372.15420954
115. 372.1+3358(from 371.3358)=372.13358
116. 372.357+043 (Special sub-divisions under 372.3-372.8, vol. 2: 836) =372.357043
117. 373.1 +623 (from 371.1-371.8)+0218(T1)+54(T2) =373.1623021854
118. 373.1 +335 +0954=373.13350954
119. 378.17+35 (from 371.32-371.39 where AVs are 371.335) =378.1735
120. 372.1(from 372.11-.18)+716 (from 371.716) = 372.1716
121. 398.2452+967 (from 592-599, where the elephant is 599.67) =398.2452967
122. 398.2492+967(from 599.67 elephants)+1(as under 592- 599 p.1228, vol.2) +513(from 591.513 Animal intelligence) = 398.24929671513
123. 398.368+3734+1(as under 583-588)+634(from581.634) (from 582-588 where rose is 583.734) = 398.36837341634
124. 523.98+6 (from 523.43-523.48 where Saturn is 523.46)

=523.986

125. 523.98+6+3(from 523.33 orbit)=523.9863
126. 529.32+45 (from 292-299 where the Hindu religion is 294.5)=529.3245
127. 539.737+62 (from 539.7211-539.7217 where mesons are 539.72162) =539.73762
128. 546.396+5 (special subdivision under 546 vol. 2, p. 1066) +88 (from 541.33-541.39)=546.396588
129. 547.1+36 (from 541.36) =547.136
130. 547.1+3884 (from 541.2-547.7)=547.13884
131. 547.01+045 (special subdivisions under 547)+884 (from 541.3884) =547.01045884
132. 547.61+045+884 (from 541.33-541.39) =547.61045884
133. 572.36+2(as under 571-572, from 571.2) =572.362
134. 572+2(from 571.2)+6(from 586 Cryptogamia)=572.26
135. 571.4+2(as under 571-572, from 571 .2)+6(from 586)=571.426
136. 572.36+2(from 571.2)+6(from 586)=572.3626
137. 572+1(as under 571-572, from 571.1) =572.1+05=572.105
138. 572.36+1(from 571.1)=572.361
139. 572.565+1(from 571.1 as given under 572.5-572.8) =572.5651
140. 572.6+1(from 571.1)=572.61
141. 572.579+1 (from 571.1)+2(from 592)=572.57912 142
142. 572.565+1(from 571.1 as under 572.5-572.8) +57(from 595.7)= 572.565157
143. 572+1(from 571.1) +57(from 595.7)+1(as under 592-599)+468 (from 591.468) =572. 1571468
144. 572.36+1(from 571.1) +5726 (from 595.726) =572.3615726

145. 572.7+1(from 571.1)+5726(from 595.726) =572.715726
146. 612.9+1 (from 611.91-611.98 where the head is 611.91) =612.91
147. 615.31+5 (from 547.01-547.08 where organometallic compounds is 547.05)=615.315
148. 615.31+61 (from 547.01-547.08 where sulfide compounds is 547.061)=615.3161
149. 615.31+5+673 (Following 546 in 546.38-546.72, where aluminium is 546.673)=615.315673
150. 615.31+5+383 (from 546.38-546.72 where potassium is 546.383) =615.315383
151. 615.925+652 (from 546.2-546.7 -where copper is 546.652) =615.925652
152. 615.925+688+24(as under 546) =615.92568824
153. 616.24+07 (as instructed under 616.1-616.9 where pathology is 07)+5(from 616.071-616.079 where diagnosis is 616.075)=616.24075
154. 616.24+07+543(from 616.07543)=616.2407543
155. 616.912 Smallpox is an asterisked class; at the footnote we have been asked to add special subject divisions as instructed under 616.1-616.9(v3:84-88). There therapies is 06; and to specify various therapies, we have been asked to add to 06 the digits following 615.8 in 615.82-615.89, and spurious therapies is 615.856. Hence,

    616.912+06+56=616.9120656
156. 616.71 +06+80902(from 615.880902)=616.710680902
157. 616.722+06+515 (from 615.8515)=616.72206515
158. 616.995+06+34(from615.834)=616.9950634
159. Tuberculosis is 616.995; for tuberculosis of a specific organ, we have been asked to divide 616.995 like

611.1-611.9, where bone is 611.71, hence the class number for bone TB is 616.995+71=616.99571

The special subject subdivisions given under

616.1-616.8 are still applicable here. Hence:

616.99571+06+34=616.995710634 is the required number.

160. 616.995+71 (from 611.1-611.9 as under 616.9953-.9959)+07(special subdivisions under 616.1- 616.9) +572 (from 616.071-616.079) =616.9957107572
161. 617.15+2(from 611.711-611.718 where ribs is 611.712) =617.152
162. 617.63+061 (from special divisions under 617) =617.63061
163. 617.632+06+45 (from 615.82-615.89 where electrotherapy is 615.845)=617.6320645
164. 618.920 (from 618.92001-618.92009) + 09 (from special sub divisions under 616.1-616.9, where case histories is 09)=618.92009
165. 621.322+76 (from 725-728 where museum buildings is 727.6)=621.32276
166. 621.322+76+5 (from 011-999) =621.322765
167. 621.322+76+570 (from 001-999 where biology is 570)+04 (as under 721-729)+72 (from 720.472) =621.32276570472
168. 621.322+5822+ (Theater is 725.822)=621.3225822
169. 621.322+782 (from 725-728 where general libraries is 727.82)+662 (from 027.1-027.8 where hospital libraries is 027.662)=621.322782662
170. 624.153+36(from 620.12-620.19 where concrete is 620.136)=624.15336
171. 624.153+36 (concrete)+72 (from 620.11272 as under 612.12-612.19, p.174, vol.3)=624.1533672

172. 630.2 (from 630.21-29) +40 (from 510-590)=630.24
173. 630.2+413 (from 510-590 where physical chemistry is 541.3)=630.2413
174. 634.04+89 (from special subdivisions under 633-635 as per instruction on page v3:307)=634.0489
175. 634.04+89+42 (from 631.81—631.89) where nitrate fertilizer is 631.842)=634.048942
176. 634.304+89+42=634.3048942
177. 635.91+842 (from 631.2-631.8)=635.91842
178. 636.50+855 (from 636.01-636.08 where feed is 636.0855)= 636.50855
179. 639.39+6 (from 597.92-597.98 where snakes is 597.96)= 639.396
180. 638.57+89 (from 595.789) =638.5789
181. 639.396+09548=639.39609548
182. 641.3 (from 641.33-.35)+31 (from 633-635 where cereals is 633.1) =641.331
183. 646.45+0 (as from 01-06 under 646.42-646.48) +4(from 646.404) =646.4504
184. 649.15+3 (from 371.91-371.95; 371.93)=649.153
185. 649.15+12(from 371.912)=649.1512
186. 649.157+924 (from Table 5 for Jews) =649.157924
187. 649.157924+0+73=649.157924073
188. 649.157+9142+0+71=649.1579142071
189. 657.8322+0+42 (from 657.1-657.7 where cost accounting is 657.42)=657.8322042
190. 657.835+0+42=657.835042
191. 657.8322+0(as under 657.8, p.400, vol.3)+42 =657.8322042
192. 661.0+711(from 546.4-546.7 where nitrogen is 546.711)+2 (as under 546,p.1066, vol.2) =661.07112

193. 660.29+6(from 541.33-541.39 where thermo chemistry is 541.36) =660.296
194. 662.622+6(from 553.21-553.25 where graphite coal is 553.26) =662.6226
195. 663.20+5 (from 663.11-663.19 where pasteurization is 663.15) =663.205
196. 666.3+5(from ss 01-09)=666.35

     It is a rare exception where a standard subdivision has been added without its featured zero.
197. 666.3+72(from ss 072) =666.372
198. 666.3+72+0+73(area) =666.372073
199. 666.3+6+0+54=666.36054
200. 667.3+39(from 677.1-677.5 where silk is 677.39)=667.339
201. 667.3+4743 (from 677.4743)=667.34743
202. 668.62+41 (from 631.83-631.85 where urea is 631.841) =668.6241
203. 668.62+42=668.6242
204. 669.96+3(from 669.1-669.7 where brass is 669.3)= 669.963
205. 669.96+7332=669.967332
206. 681.414+4 (from 535.842-535.846 where ultraviolet light is 535.844) =681.4144
207. 681.414+2+028 (T1)=681.4142028
208. 681.8+787 (from 786-788 where the guitar is 787.87) =681.8787
209. 681.8+62+1(as under 18-19 of 784-788)+928 (from 784.1928) =681.8621928
210. 688.76+355(from 796.1-796.9 where field hockey is 796.355)=688.76355
211. 688.76+91 (from 796.91)=688.7691

212. 697.9 (from 697.95-.98) +76 (from 725-728 where museum buildings is 727.6) =697.976
213. 697.9+76+570 (from 001-999 where biology is 570) =697.97657
214. 697.9+782(from 725-728 where general libraries is 727.82)+662 (from 027.1-027.8 where hospital libraries is 027.662)=697.9782662
215. 697.9+8=697.98
216. 697.9+8 (from 728) +04 (as under 721-729) +83 (from 720.483) =697.980483
217. 704.9489+43 (following 29 in 292-299, where Buddhism is 294.3) =704.948943
218. 704.949+61 (from 000-999)=704.94961
219. 721.0447+142(from 669.1-669.7, where steel is 669.142) =721.0447142
220. 725.84+087(from T1)=725.84087
221. 725.83+04(as under 721-729)+9(from 720.49) =725.83049
222. 726.1+45(from 292-299 where Hinduism is 294.5) = 726.145
223. 727.4+02(from 001-999)=727.402

     Whereas the architecture of library buildings is placed at 727.8 which is amenable to further expansion.
224. 727.82
225. 727.82+662(from 027.662)=727.82662
226. 727.82+662+0286(v3:555)=727.826620286
227. 728.373 + 04(as under 721-729) + 72 (from 720.472) = 728.3730472
228. 727.82+5(from 027.5)+54(Area Table)+010(at 721-729) +3(from 700.103)=727.825540103
229. 728.4+0846 (T1,Std sub)=728.40846

230. 743.8+36(from 704.9436)+ 54(T2) =743.83654
231. 743.6+847 (from 592-599 where penguins is 598.47)=743.6847
232. 758.9+954(from 001-999)=758.9954
233. 758.9+954.025=758.9954025
234. 777.8+32(from 704.9432)+8 (from 598)+0285 =777.83280285
235. 779+32(from 704.9432)+8(from 598)=779.328
236. 799.17+3 (from 597.2-597.7, where sharks is 597.3) =799.173
237. 781.7+46 (from 294-299 where Sikhism is 294.6) =781.746
238. 781.7+46 (from 294.6) +0 (as under 784.74-784.79) +52 (from 781.52) =781.746052
239. 784.2+078 (from 784-744 and 780.78) + 421 (T2) 784.2078421
240. 787.20266 (from 780.266)
241. 909.4+91425 (T5) +82 (from 909.82) =909.49142582
242. 91+545 (T2) +04 (as under 913-919)+31 (from 954.031) =915.450431
243. 9+5478 (T2) +003 (as under 930-990) =954.78003

Index

Names of subjects denote their classification
All concepts are in context of DDC23
Abbreviations used;
DDC = Dewey Decimal Classification
RI = Relative Index
ss = Standard Subdivisions